ISBN 0-8373-2152-2

C-2152   CAREER EXAMINATION SERIES

This is your PASSBOOK® for...

Sanitation Inspector

Test Preparation Study Guide

Questions & Answers

NATIONAL LEARNING CORPORATION

Copyright © 2012 by

National Learning Corporation

212 Michael Drive, Syosset, New York 11791

(516) 921-8888
(800) 645-6337
FAX: (516) 921-8743
www.passbooks.com
sales @ passbooks.com
info @ passbooks.com

PRINTED IN THE UNITED STATES OF AMERICA

PASSBOOK®
NOTICE

PASSBOOK® SERIES

THE *PASSBOOK® SERIES* has been created to prepare applicants and candidates for the ultimate academic battlefield — the examination room.

At some time in our lives, each and every one of us may be required to take an examination — for validation, matriculation, admission, qualification, registration, certification, or licensure.

Based on the assumption that every applicant or candidate has met the basic formal educational standards, has taken the required number of courses, and read the necessary texts, the *PASSBOOK® SERIES* furnishes the one special preparation which may assure passing with confidence, instead of failing with insecurity. Examination questions — together with answers — are furnished as the basic vehicle for study so that the mysteries of the examination and its compounding difficulties may be eliminated or diminished by a sure method.

This book is meant to help you pass your examination provided that you qualify and are serious in your objective.

The entire field is reviewed through the huge store of content information which is succinctly presented through a provocative and challenging approach — the question-and-answer method.

A climate of success is established by furnishing the correct answers at the end of each test.

You soon learn to recognize types of questions, forms of questions, and patterns of questioning. You may even begin to anticipate expected outcomes.

You perceive that many questions are repeated or adapted so that you can gain acute insights, which may enable you to score many sure points.

You learn how to confront new questions, or types of questions, and to attack them confidently and work out the correct answers.

You note objectives and emphases, and recognize pitfalls and dangers, so that you may make positive educational adjustments.

Moreover, you are kept fully informed in relation to new concepts, methods, practices, and directions in the field.

You discover that you are actually taking the examination all the time: you are preparing for the examination by "taking" an examination, not by reading extraneous and/or supererogatory textbooks.

In short, this PASSBOOK®, used directedly, should be an important factor in helping you to pass your test.

SANITATION INSPECTOR

DUTIES
Performs routine inspections of residences and business establishments in order to ensure compliance with established codes and regulations. The incumbent is required to inspect refuse collection work performed by private companies under contract with a municipality, to determine if the work is being performed in accordance with the established contractual agreement. Responsibility may be included for assignment to a landfill transfer station to inspect loads of general refuse and construction and demolition material for compliance with regulations. Work is performed under the general supervision of assigned supervisory personnel, and is reviewed through oral and written reports and by occasional field visits. Does related work as required.

SCOPE OF THE EXAMINATION
The written test will cover knowledge, skills and/or abilities in such areas as:

1. Preparing written material;
2. Principles of litter and garbage control;
3. Principles and practices of sanitary inspection; and
4. Understanding and interpreting written material.

HOW TO TAKE A TEST

I. YOU MUST PASS AN EXAMINATION

A. WHAT EVERY CANDIDATE SHOULD KNOW

Examination applicants often ask us for help in preparing for the written test. What can I study in advance? What kinds of questions will be asked? How will the test be given? How will the papers be graded?

As an applicant for a civil service examination, you may be wondering about some of these things. Our purpose here is to suggest effective methods of advance study and to describe civil service examinations.

Your chances for success on this examination can be increased if you know how to prepare. Those "pre-examination jitters" can be reduced if you know what to expect. You can even experience an adventure in good citizenship if you know why civil service exams are given.

B. WHY ARE CIVIL SERVICE EXAMINATIONS GIVEN?

Civil service examinations are important to you in two ways. As a citizen, you want public jobs filled by employees who know how to do their work. As a job seeker, you want a fair chance to compete for that job on an equal footing with other candidates. The best-known means of accomplishing this two-fold goal is the competitive examination.

Exams are widely publicized throughout the nation. They may be administered for jobs in federal, state, city, municipal, town or village governments or agencies.

Any citizen may apply, with some limitations, such as the age or residence of applicants. Your experience and education may be reviewed to see whether you meet the requirements for the particular examination. When these requirements exist, they are reasonable and applied consistently to all applicants. Thus, a competitive examination may cause you some uneasiness now, but it is your privilege and safeguard.

C. HOW ARE CIVIL SERVICE EXAMS DEVELOPED?

Examinations are carefully written by trained technicians who are specialists in the field known as "psychological measurement," in consultation with recognized authorities in the field of work that the test will cover. These experts recommend the subject matter areas or skills to be tested; only those knowledges or skills important to your success on the job are included. The most reliable books and source materials available are used as references. Together, the experts and technicians judge the difficulty level of the questions.

Test technicians know how to phrase questions so that the problem is clearly stated. Their ethics do not permit "trick" or "catch" questions. Questions may have been tried out on sample groups, or subjected to statistical analysis, to determine their usefulness.

Written tests are often used in combination with performance tests, ratings of training and experience, and oral interviews. All of these measures combine to form the best-known means of finding the right person for the right job.

II. HOW TO PASS THE WRITTEN TEST

A. NATURE OF THE EXAMINATION

To prepare intelligently for civil service examinations, you should know how they differ from school examinations you have taken. In school you were assigned certain definite pages to read or subjects to cover. The examination questions were quite detailed and usually emphasized memory. Civil service exams, on the other hand, try to discover your present ability to perform the duties of a position, plus your potentiality to learn these duties. In other words, a civil service exam attempts to predict how successful you will be. Questions cover such a broad area that they cannot be as minute and detailed as school exam questions.

In the public service similar kinds of work, or positions, are grouped together in one "class." This process is known as *position-classification*. All the positions in a class are paid according to the salary range for that class. One class title covers all of these positions, and they are all tested by the same examination.

B. FOUR BASIC STEPS

1) Study the announcement

How, then, can you know what subjects to study? Our best answer is: "Learn as much as possible about the class of positions for which you've applied." The exam will test the knowledge, skills and abilities needed to do the work.

Your most valuable source of information about the position you want is the official exam announcement. This announcement lists the training and experience qualifications. Check these standards and apply only if you come reasonably close to meeting them.

The brief description of the position in the examination announcement offers some clues to the subjects which will be tested. Think about the job itself. Review the duties in your mind. Can you perform them, or are there some in which you are rusty? Fill in the blank spots in your preparation.

Many jurisdictions preview the written test in the exam announcement by including a section called "Knowledge and Abilities Required," "Scope of the Examination," or some similar heading. Here you will find out specifically what fields will be tested.

2) Review your own background

Once you learn in general what the position is all about, and what you need to know to do the work, ask yourself which subjects you already know fairly well and which need improvement. You may wonder whether to concentrate on improving your strong areas or on building some background in your fields of weakness. When the announcement has specified "some knowledge" or "considerable knowledge," or has used adjectives like "beginning principles of..." or "advanced ... methods," you can get a clue as to the number and difficulty of questions to be asked in any given field. More questions, and hence broader coverage, would be included for those subjects which are more important in the work. Now weigh your strengths and weaknesses against the job requirements and prepare accordingly.

3) Determine the level of the position

Another way to tell how intensively you should prepare is to understand the level of the job for which you are applying. Is it the entering level? In other words, is this the position in which beginners in a field of work are hired? Or is it an intermediate or advanced level? Sometimes this is indicated by such words as "Junior" or "Senior" in the class title. Other jurisdictions use Roman numerals to designate the level – Clerk I, Clerk II, for example. The word "Supervisor" sometimes appears in the title. If the level is not indicated by the title, check the description of duties. Will you be working under very close supervision, or will you have responsibility for independent decisions in this work?

4) Choose appropriate study materials

Now that you know the subjects to be examined and the relative amount of each subject to be covered, you can choose suitable study materials. For beginning level jobs, or even advanced ones, if you have a pronounced weakness in some aspect of your training, read a modern, standard textbook in that field. Be sure it is up to date and has general coverage. Such books are normally available at your library, and the librarian will be glad to help you locate one. For entry-level positions, questions of appropriate difficulty are chosen – neither highly advanced questions, nor those too simple. Such questions require careful thought but not advanced training.

If the position for which you are applying is technical or advanced, you will read more advanced, specialized material. If you are already familiar with the basic principles of your field, elementary textbooks would waste your time. Concentrate on advanced textbooks and technical periodicals. Think through the concepts and review difficult problems in your field.

These are all general sources. You can get more ideas on your own initiative, following these leads. For example, training manuals and publications of the government agency which employs workers in your field can be useful, particularly for technical and professional positions. A letter or visit to the government department involved may result in more specific study suggestions, and certainly will provide you with a more definite idea of the exact nature of the position you are seeking.

III. KINDS OF TESTS

Tests are used for purposes other than measuring knowledge and ability to perform specified duties. For some positions, it is equally important to test ability to make adjustments to new situations or to profit from training. In others, basic mental abilities not dependent on information are essential. Questions which test these things may not appear as pertinent to the duties of the position as those which test for knowledge and information. Yet they are often highly important parts of a fair examination. For very general questions, it is almost impossible to help you direct your study efforts. What we can do is to point out some of the more common of these general abilities needed in public service positions and describe some typical questions.

1) General information

Broad, general information has been found useful for predicting job success in some kinds of work. This is tested in a variety of ways, from vocabulary lists to questions about current events. Basic background in some field of work, such as sociology or economics, may be sampled in a group of questions. Often these are principles which have become familiar to most persons through exposure rather than through formal training. It is difficult to advise you how to study for these questions; being alert to the world around you is our best suggestion.

2) Verbal ability

An example of an ability needed in many positions is verbal or language ability. Verbal ability is, in brief, the ability to use and understand words. Vocabulary and grammar tests are typical measures of this ability. Reading comprehension or paragraph interpretation questions are common in many kinds of civil service tests. You are given a paragraph of written material and asked to find its central meaning.

3) Numerical ability

Number skills can be tested by the familiar arithmetic problem, by checking paired lists of numbers to see which are alike and which are different, or by interpreting charts and graphs. In the latter test, a graph may be printed in the test booklet which you are asked to use as the basis for answering questions.

4) Observation

A popular test for law-enforcement positions is the observation test. A picture is shown to you for several minutes, then taken away. Questions about the picture test your ability to observe both details and larger elements.

5) Following directions

In many positions in the public service, the employee must be able to carry out written instructions dependably and accurately. You may be given a chart with several columns, each column listing a variety of information. The questions require you to carry out directions involving the information given in the chart.

6) Skills and aptitudes

Performance tests effectively measure some manual skills and aptitudes. When the skill is one in which you are trained, such as typing or shorthand, you can practice. These tests are often very much like those given in business school or high school courses. For many of the other skills and aptitudes, however, no short-time preparation can be made. Skills and abilities natural to you or that you have developed throughout your lifetime are being tested.

Many of the general questions just described provide all the data needed to answer the questions and ask you to use your reasoning ability to find the answers. Your best preparation for these tests, as well as for tests of facts and ideas, is to be at your physical and mental best. You, no doubt, have your own methods of getting into an exam-taking mood and keeping "in shape." The next section lists some ideas on this subject.

IV. KINDS OF QUESTIONS

Only rarely is the "essay" question, which you answer in narrative form, used in civil service tests. Civil service tests are usually of the short-answer type. Full instructions for answering these questions will be given to you at the examination. But in case this is your first experience with short-answer questions and separate answer sheets, here is what you need to know:

1) Multiple-choice Questions

Most popular of the short-answer questions is the "multiple choice" or "best answer" question. It can be used, for example, to test for factual knowledge, ability to solve problems or judgment in meeting situations found at work.

A multiple-choice question is normally one of three types—

- It can begin with an incomplete statement followed by several possible endings. You are to find the one ending which *best* completes the statement, although some of the others may not be entirely wrong.
- It can also be a complete statement in the form of a question which is answered by choosing one of the statements listed.
- It can be in the form of a problem – again you select the best answer.

Here is an example of a multiple-choice question with a discussion which should give you some clues as to the method for choosing the right answer:

When an employee has a complaint about his assignment, the action which will *best* help him overcome his difficulty is to

- A. discuss his difficulty with his coworkers
- B. take the problem to the head of the organization
- C. take the problem to the person who gave him the assignment
- D. say nothing to anyone about his complaint

In answering this question, you should study each of the choices to find which is best. Consider choice "A" – Certainly an employee may discuss his complaint with fellow employees, but no change or improvement can result, and the complaint remains unresolved. Choice "B" is a poor choice since the head of the organization probably does not know what assignment you have been given, and taking your problem to him is known as "going over the head" of the supervisor. The supervisor, or person who made the assignment, is the person who can clarify it or correct any injustice. Choice "C" is, therefore, correct. To say nothing, as in choice "D," is unwise. Supervisors have and interest in knowing the problems employees are facing, and the employee is seeking a solution to his problem.

2) True/False Questions

The "true/false" or "right/wrong" form of question is sometimes used. Here a complete statement is given. Your job is to decide whether the statement is right or wrong.

SAMPLE: A person-to-person long-distance telephone call costs less than a station-to-station call to the same city.

This statement is wrong, or false, since person-to-person calls are more expensive.

This is not a complete list of all possible question forms, although most of the others are variations of these common types. You will always get complete directions for answering questions. Be sure you understand *how* to mark your answers – ask questions until you do.

V. RECORDING YOUR ANSWERS

For an examination with very few applicants, you may be told to record your answers in the test booklet itself. Separate answer sheets are much more common. If this separate answer sheet is to be scored by machine – and this is often the case – it is highly important that you mark your answers correctly in order to get credit.

An electric scoring machine is often used in civil service offices because of the speed with which papers can be scored. Machine-scored answer sheets must be marked with a pencil, which will be given to you. This pencil has a high graphite content which responds to the electric scoring machine. As a matter of fact, stray dots may register as answers, so do not let your pencil rest on the answer sheet while you are pondering the correct answer. Also, if your pencil lead breaks or is otherwise defective, ask for another.

Since the answer sheet will be dropped in a slot in the scoring machine, be careful not to bend the corners or get the paper crumpled.

The answer sheet normally has five vertical columns of numbers, with 30 numbers to a column. These numbers correspond to the question numbers in your test booklet. After each number, going across the page are four or five pairs of dotted lines. These short dotted lines have small letters or numbers above them. The first two pairs may also have a "T" or "F" above the letters. This indicates that the first two pairs only are to be used if the questions are of the true-false type. If the questions are multiple choice, disregard the "T" and "F" and pay attention only to the small letters or numbers.

Answer your questions in the manner of the sample that follows:

32. The largest city in the United States is
    A. Washington, D.C.
    B. New York City
    C. Chicago
    D. Detroit
    E. San Francisco

1) Choose the answer you think is best. (New York City is the largest, so "B" is correct.)
2) Find the row of dotted lines numbered the same as the question you are answering. (Find row number 32)
3) Find the pair of dotted lines corresponding to the answer. (Find the pair of lines under the mark "B.")
4) Make a solid black mark between the dotted lines.

VI. BEFORE THE TEST

Common sense will help you find procedures to follow to get ready for an examination. Too many of us, however, overlook these sensible measures. Indeed, nervousness and fatigue have been found to be the most serious reasons why applicants fail to do their best on civil service tests. Here is a list of reminders:

- Begin your preparation early – Don't wait until the last minute to go scurrying around for books and materials or to find out what the position is all about.
- Prepare continuously – An hour a night for a week is better than an all-night cram session. This has been definitely established. What is more, a night a

6

week for a month will return better dividends than crowding your study into a shorter period of time.

- Locate the place of the exam – You have been sent a notice telling you when and where to report for the examination. If the location is in a different town or otherwise unfamiliar to you, it would be well to inquire the best route and learn something about the building.

- Relax the night before the test – Allow your mind to rest. Do not study at all that night. Plan some mild recreation or diversion; then go to bed early and get a good night's sleep.

- Get up early enough to make a leisurely trip to the place for the test – This way unforeseen events, traffic snarls, unfamiliar buildings, etc. will not upset you.

- Dress comfortably – A written test is not a fashion show. You will be known by number and not by name, so wear something comfortable.

- Leave excess paraphernalia at home – Shopping bags and odd bundles will get in your way. You need bring only the items mentioned in the official notice you received; usually everything you need is provided. Do not bring reference books to the exam. They will only confuse those last minutes and be taken away from you when in the test room.

- Arrive somewhat ahead of time – If because of transportation schedules you must get there very early, bring a newspaper or magazine to take your mind off yourself while waiting.

- Locate the examination room – When you have found the proper room, you will be directed to the seat or part of the room where you will sit. Sometimes you are given a sheet of instructions to read while you are waiting. Do not fill out any forms until you are told to do so; just read them and be prepared.

- Relax and prepare to listen to the instructions

- If you have any physical problem that may keep you from doing your best, be sure to tell the test administrator. If you are sick or in poor health, you really cannot do your best on the exam. You can come back and take the test some other time.

VII. AT THE TEST

The day of the test is here and you have the test booklet in your hand. The temptation to get going is very strong. Caution! There is more to success than knowing the right answers. You must know how to identify your papers and understand variations in the type of short-answer question used in this particular examination. Follow these suggestions for maximum results from your efforts:

1) Cooperate with the monitor

The test administrator has a duty to create a situation in which you can be as much at ease as possible. He will give instructions, tell you when to begin, check to see that you are marking your answer sheet correctly, and so on. He is not there to guard you, although he will see that your competitors do not take unfair advantage. He wants to help you do your best.

2) Listen to all instructions

Don't jump the gun! Wait until you understand all directions. In most civil service tests you get more time than you need to answer the questions. So don't be in a hurry.

Read each word of instructions until you clearly understand the meaning. Study the examples, listen to all announcements and follow directions. Ask questions if you do not understand what to do.

3) Identify your papers

Civil service exams are usually identified by number only. You will be assigned a number; you must not put your name on your test papers. Be sure to copy your number correctly. Since more than one exam may be given, copy your exact examination title.

4) Plan your time

Unless you are told that a test is a "speed" or "rate of work" test, speed itself is usually not important. Time enough to answer all the questions will be provided, but this does not mean that you have all day. An overall time limit has been set. Divide the total time (in minutes) by the number of questions to determine the approximate time you have for each question.

5) Do not linger over difficult questions

If you come across a difficult question, mark it with a paper clip (useful to have along) and come back to it when you have been through the booklet. One caution if you do this – be sure to skip a number on your answer sheet as well. Check often to be sure that you have not lost your place and that you are marking in the row numbered the same as the question you are answering.

6) Read the questions

Be sure you know what the question asks! Many capable people are unsuccessful because they failed to *read* the questions correctly.

7) Answer all questions

Unless you have been instructed that a penalty will be deducted for incorrect answers, it is better to guess than to omit a question.

8) Speed tests

It is often better NOT to guess on speed tests. It has been found that on timed tests people are tempted to spend the last few seconds before time is called in marking answers at random – without even reading them – in the hope of picking up a few extra points. To discourage this practice, the instructions may warn you that your score will be "corrected" for guessing. That is, a penalty will be applied. The incorrect answers will be deducted from the correct ones, or some other penalty formula will be used.

9) Review your answers

If you finish before time is called, go back to the questions you guessed or omitted to give them further thought. Review other answers if you have time.

10) Return your test materials

If you are ready to leave before others have finished or time is called, take ALL your materials to the monitor and leave quietly. Never take any test material with you. The monitor can discover whose papers are not complete, and taking a test booklet may be grounds for disqualification.

VIII. EXAMINATION TECHNIQUES

1) Read the general instructions carefully. These are usually printed on the first page of the exam booklet. As a rule, these instructions refer to the timing of the examination; the fact that you should not start work until the signal and must stop work at a signal, etc. If there are any *special* instructions, such as a choice of questions to be answered, make sure that you note this instruction carefully.

2) When you are ready to start work on the examination, that is as soon as the signal has been given, read the instructions to each question booklet, underline any key words or phrases, such as *least, best, outline, describe* and the like. In this way you will tend to answer as requested rather than discover on reviewing your paper that you *listed without describing*, that you selected the *worst* choice rather than the *best* choice, etc.

3) If the examination is of the objective or multiple-choice type – that is, each question will also give a series of possible answers: A, B, C or D, and you are called upon to select the best answer and write the letter next to that answer on your answer paper – it is advisable to start answering each question in turn. There may be anywhere from 50 to 100 such questions in the three or four hours allotted and you can see how much time would be taken if you read through all the questions before beginning to answer any. Furthermore, if you come across a question or group of questions which you know would be difficult to answer, it would undoubtedly affect your handling of all the other questions.

4) If the examination is of the essay type and contains but a few questions, it is a moot point as to whether you should read all the questions before starting to answer any one. Of course, if you are given a choice – say five out of seven and the like – then it is essential to read all the questions so you can eliminate the two that are most difficult. If, however, you are asked to answer all the questions, there may be danger in trying to answer the easiest one first because you may find that you will spend too much time on it. The best technique is to answer the first question, then proceed to the second, etc.

5) Time your answers. Before the exam begins, write down the time it started, then add the time allowed for the examination and write down the time it must be completed, then divide the time available somewhat as follows:
   - If 3-1/2 hours are allowed, that would be 210 minutes. If you have 80 objective-type questions, that would be an average of 2-1/2 minutes per question. Allow yourself no more than 2 minutes per question, or a total of 160 minutes, which will permit about 50 minutes to review.
   - If for the time allotment of 210 minutes there are 7 essay questions to answer, that would average about 30 minutes a question. Give yourself only 25 minutes per question so that you have about 35 minutes to review.

6) The most important instruction is to *read each question* and make sure you know what is wanted. The second most important instruction is to *time yourself properly* so that you answer every question. The third most

important instruction is to *answer every question.* Guess if you have to but include something for each question. Remember that you will receive no credit for a blank and will probably receive some credit if you write something in answer to an essay question. If you guess a letter – say "B" for a multiple-choice question – you may have guessed right. If you leave a blank as an answer to a multiple-choice question, the examiners may respect your feelings but it will not add a point to your score. Some exams may penalize you for wrong answers, so in such cases *only*, you may not want to guess unless you have some basis for your answer.

7) Suggestions
   a. Objective-type questions
      1. Examine the question booklet for proper sequence of pages and questions
      2. Read all instructions carefully
      3. Skip any question which seems too difficult; return to it after all other questions have been answered
      4. Apportion your time properly; do not spend too much time on any single question or group of questions
      5. Note and underline key words – *all, most, fewest, least, best, worst, same, opposite,* etc.
      6. Pay particular attention to negatives
      7. Note unusual option, e.g., unduly long, short, complex, different or similar in content to the body of the question
      8. Observe the use of "hedging" words – *probably, may, most likely,* etc.
      9. Make sure that your answer is put next to the same number as the question
      10. Do not second-guess unless you have good reason to believe the second answer is definitely more correct
      11. Cross out original answer if you decide another answer is more accurate; do not erase until you are ready to hand your paper in
      12. Answer all questions; guess unless instructed otherwise
      13. Leave time for review

   b. Essay questions
      1. Read each question carefully
      2. Determine exactly what is wanted. Underline key words or phrases.
      3. Decide on outline or paragraph answer
      4. Include many different points and elements unless asked to develop any one or two points or elements
      5. Show impartiality by giving pros and cons unless directed to select one side only
      6. Make and write down any assumptions you find necessary to answer the questions
      7. Watch your English, grammar, punctuation and choice of words
      8. Time your answers; don't crowd material

8) Answering the essay question

Most essay questions can be answered by framing the specific response around several key words or ideas. Here are a few such key words or ideas:

M's: manpower, materials, methods, money, management
P's: purpose, program, policy, plan, procedure, practice, problems, pitfalls, personnel, public relations

    a. Six basic steps in handling problems:
1. Preliminary plan and background development
2. Collect information, data and facts
3. Analyze and interpret information, data and facts
4. Analyze and develop solutions as well as make recommendations
5. Prepare report and sell recommendations
6. Install recommendations and follow up effectiveness

    b. Pitfalls to avoid
1. *Taking things for granted* – A statement of the situation does not necessarily imply that each of the elements is necessarily true; for example, a complaint may be invalid and biased so that all that can be taken for granted is that a complaint has been registered
2. *Considering only one side of a situation* – Wherever possible, indicate several alternatives and then point out the reasons you selected the best one
3. *Failing to indicate follow up* – Whenever your answer indicates action on your part, make certain that you will take proper follow-up action to see how successful your recommendations, procedures or actions turn out to be
4. *Taking too long in answering any single question* – Remember to time your answers properly

IX. AFTER THE TEST

Scoring procedures differ in detail among civil service jurisdictions although the general principles are the same. Whether the papers are hand-scored or graded by machine we have described, they are nearly always graded by number. That is, the person who marks the paper knows only the number – never the name – of the applicant. Not until all the papers have been graded will they be matched with names. If other tests, such as training and experience or oral interview ratings have been given, scores will be combined. Different parts of the examination usually have different weights. For example, the written test might count 60 percent of the final grade, and a rating of training and experience 40 percent. In many jurisdictions, veterans will have a certain number of points added to their grades.

After the final grade has been determined, the names are placed in grade order and an eligible list is established. There are various methods for resolving ties between those who get the same final grade – probably the most common is to place first the name of the person whose application was received first. Job offers are made from the eligible list in the order the names appear on it. You will be notified of your grade and your rank as soon as all these computations have been made. This will be done as rapidly as possible.

People who are found to meet the requirements in the announcement are called "eligibles." Their names are put on a list of eligible candidates. An eligible's chances of getting a job depend on how high he stands on this list and how fast agencies are filling jobs from the list.

When a job is to be filled from a list of eligibles, the agency asks for the names of people on the list of eligibles for that job. When the civil service commission receives this request, it sends to the agency the names of the three people highest on this list. Or, if the job to be filled has specialized requirements, the office sends the agency the names of the top three persons who meet these requirements from the general list.

The appointing officer makes a choice from among the three people whose names were sent to him. If the selected person accepts the appointment, the names of the others are put back on the list to be considered for future openings.

That is the rule in hiring from all kinds of eligible lists, whether they are for typist, carpenter, chemist, or something else. For every vacancy, the appointing officer has his choice of any one of the top three eligibles on the list. This explains why the person whose name is on top of the list sometimes does not get an appointment when some of the persons lower on the list do. If the appointing officer chooses the second or third eligible, the No. 1 eligible does not get a job at once, but stays on the list until he is appointed or the list is terminated.

X. HOW TO PASS THE INTERVIEW TEST

The examination for which you applied requires an oral interview test. You have already taken the written test and you are now being called for the interview test – the final part of the formal examination.

You may think that it is not possible to prepare for an interview test and that there are no procedures to follow during an interview. Our purpose is to point out some things you can do in advance that will help you and some good rules to follow and pitfalls to avoid while you are being interviewed.

What is an interview supposed to test?

The written examination is designed to test the technical knowledge and competence of the candidate; the oral is designed to evaluate intangible qualities, not readily measured otherwise, and to establish a list showing the relative fitness of each candidate – as measured against his competitors – for the position sought. Scoring is not on the basis of "right" and "wrong," but on a sliding scale of values ranging from "not passable" to "outstanding." As a matter of fact, it is possible to achieve a relatively low score without a single "incorrect" answer because of evident weakness in the qualities being measured.

Occasionally, an examination may consist entirely of an oral test – either an individual or a group oral. In such cases, information is sought concerning the technical knowledges and abilities of the candidate, since there has been no written examination for this purpose. More commonly, however, an oral test is used to supplement a written examination.

Who conducts interviews?

The composition of oral boards varies among different jurisdictions. In nearly all, a representative of the personnel department serves as chairman. One of the members of the board may be a representative of the department in which the candidate would work. In some cases, "outside experts" are used, and, frequently, a businessman or some other representative of the general public is asked to serve. Labor and management or other special groups may be represented. The aim is to secure the services of experts in the appropriate field.

However the board is composed, it is a good idea (and not at all improper or unethical) to ascertain in advance of the interview who the members are and what groups they represent. When you are introduced to them, you will have some idea of their backgrounds and interests, and at least you will not stutter and stammer over their names.

What should be done before the interview?

While knowledge about the board members is useful and takes some of the surprise element out of the interview, there is other preparation which is more substantive. It *is* possible to prepare for an oral interview – in several ways:

1) Keep a copy of your application and review it carefully before the interview

This may be the only document before the oral board, and the starting point of the interview. Know what education and experience you have listed there, and the sequence and dates of all of it. Sometimes the board will ask you to review the highlights of your experience for them; you should not have to hem and haw doing it.

2) Study the class specification and the examination announcement

Usually, the oral board has one or both of these to guide them. The qualities, characteristics or knowledges required by the position sought are stated in these documents. They offer valuable clues as to the nature of the oral interview. For example, if the job involves supervisory responsibilities, the announcement will usually indicate that knowledge of modern supervisory methods and the qualifications of the candidate as a supervisor will be tested. If so, you can expect such questions, frequently in the form of a hypothetical situation which you are expected to solve. NEVER go into an oral without knowledge of the duties and responsibilities of the job you seek.

3) Think-through each qualification required

Try to visualize the kind of questions you would ask if you were a board member. How well could you answer them? Try especially to appraise your own knowledge and background in each area, *measured against the job sought*, and identify any areas in which you are weak. Be critical and realistic – do not flatter yourself.

4) Do some general reading in areas in which you feel you may be weak

For example, if the job involves supervision and your past experience has NOT, some general reading in supervisory methods and practices, particularly in the field of human relations, might be useful. Do NOT study agency procedures or detailed manuals. The oral board will be testing your understanding and capacity, not your memory.

5) Get a good night's sleep and watch your general health and mental attitude

You will want a clear head at the interview. Take care of a cold or any other minor ailment, and of course, no hangovers.

What should be done on the day of the interview?

Now comes the day of the interview itself. Give yourself plenty of time to get there. Plan to arrive somewhat ahead of the scheduled time, particularly if your appointment is in the fore part of the day. If a previous candidate fails to appear, the board might be ready for you a bit early. By early afternoon an oral board is almost invariably behind schedule if there are many candidates, and you may have to wait.

Take along a book or magazine to read, or your application to review, but leave any extraneous material in the waiting room when you go in for your interview. In any event, relax and compose yourself.

The matter of dress is important. The board is forming impressions about you – from your experience, your manners, your attitude, and your appearance. Give your personal appearance careful attention. Dress your best, but not your flashiest. Choose conservative, appropriate clothing, and be sure it is immaculate. This is a business interview, and your appearance should indicate that you regard it as such. Besides, being well groomed and properly dressed will help boost your confidence.

Sooner or later, someone will call your name and escort you into the interview room. *This is it.* From here on you are on your own. It is too late for any more preparation. But remember, you asked for this opportunity to prove your fitness, and you are here because your request was granted.

What happens when you go in?

The usual sequence of events will be as follows: The clerk (who is often the board stenographer) will introduce you to the chairman of the oral board, who will introduce you to the other members of the board. Acknowledge the introductions before you sit down. Do not be surprised if you find a microphone facing you or a stenotypist sitting by. Oral interviews are usually recorded in the event of an appeal or other review.

Usually the chairman of the board will open the interview by reviewing the highlights of your education and work experience from your application – primarily for the benefit of the other members of the board, as well as to get the material into the record. Do not interrupt or comment unless there is an error or significant misinterpretation; if that is the case, do not hesitate. But do not quibble about insignificant matters. Also, he will usually ask you some question about your education, experience or your present job – partly to get you to start talking and to establish the interviewing "rapport." He may start the actual questioning, or turn it over to one of the other members. Frequently, each member undertakes the questioning on a particular area, one in which he is perhaps most competent, so you can expect each member to participate in the examination. Because time is limited, you may also expect some rather abrupt switches in the direction the questioning takes, so do not be upset by it. Normally, a board member will not pursue a single line of questioning unless he discovers a particular strength or weakness.

After each member has participated, the chairman will usually ask whether any member has any further questions, then will ask you if you have anything you wish to add. Unless you are expecting this question, it may floor you. Worse, it may start you off on an extended, extemporaneous speech. The board is not usually seeking more information. The question is principally to offer you a last opportunity to present further qualifications or to indicate that you have nothing to add. So, if you feel that a significant qualification or characteristic has been overlooked, it is proper to point it out in a sentence or so. Do not compliment the board on the thoroughness of their examination – they have been sketchy, and you know it. If you wish, merely say, "No thank you, I have nothing further to add." This is a point where you can "talk yourself out" of a good impression or fail to present an important bit of information. Remember, *you close the interview yourself.*

The chairman will then say, "That is all, Mr. _____, thank you." Do not be startled; the interview is over, and quicker than you think. Thank him, gather your belongings and take your leave. Save your sigh of relief for the other side of the door.

How to put your best foot forward

Throughout this entire process, you may feel that the board individually and collectively is trying to pierce your defenses, seek out your hidden weaknesses and embarrass and confuse you. Actually, this is not true. They are obliged to make an appraisal of your qualifications for the job you are seeking, and they want to see you in your best light. Remember, they must interview all candidates and a non-cooperative candidate may become a failure in spite of their best efforts to bring out his qualifications. Here are 15 suggestions that will help you:

1) Be natural – Keep your attitude confident, not cocky

If you are not confident that you can do the job, do not expect the board to be. Do not apologize for your weaknesses, try to bring out your strong points. The board is interested in a positive, not negative, presentation. Cockiness will antagonize any board member and make him wonder if you are covering up a weakness by a false show of strength.

2) Get comfortable, but don't lounge or sprawl

Sit erectly but not stiffly. A careless posture may lead the board to conclude that you are careless in other things, or at least that you are not impressed by the importance of the occasion. Either conclusion is natural, even if incorrect. Do not fuss with your clothing, a pencil or an ashtray. Your hands may occasionally be useful to emphasize a point; do not let them become a point of distraction.

3) Do not wisecrack or make small talk

This is a serious situation, and your attitude should show that you consider it as such. Further, the time of the board is limited – they do not want to waste it, and neither should you.

4) Do not exaggerate your experience or abilities

In the first place, from information in the application or other interviews and sources, the board may know more about you than you think. Secondly, you probably will not get away with it. An experienced board is rather adept at spotting such a situation, so do not take the chance.

5) If you know a board member, do not make a point of it, yet do not hide it

Certainly you are not fooling him, and probably not the other members of the board. Do not try to take advantage of your acquaintanceship – it will probably do you little good.

6) Do not dominate the interview

Let the board do that. They will give you the clues – do not assume that you have to do all the talking. Realize that the board has a number of questions to ask you, and do not try to take up all the interview time by showing off your extensive knowledge of the answer to the first one.

7) Be attentive

You only have 20 minutes or so, and you should keep your attention at its sharpest throughout. When a member is addressing a problem or question to you, give him your undivided attention. Address your reply principally to him, but do not exclude the other board members.

8) Do not interrupt

A board member may be stating a problem for you to analyze. He will ask you a question when the time comes. Let him state the problem, and wait for the question.

9) Make sure you understand the question

Do not try to answer until you are sure what the question is. If it is not clear, restate it in your own words or ask the board member to clarify it for you. However, do not haggle about minor elements.

10) Reply promptly but not hastily

A common entry on oral board rating sheets is "candidate responded readily," or "candidate hesitated in replies." Respond as promptly and quickly as you can, but do not jump to a hasty, ill-considered answer.

11) Do not be peremptory in your answers

A brief answer is proper – but do not fire your answer back. That is a losing game from your point of view. The board member can probably ask questions much faster than you can answer them.

12) Do not try to create the answer you think the board member wants

He is interested in what kind of mind you have and how it works – not in playing games. Furthermore, he can usually spot this practice and will actually grade you down on it.

13) Do not switch sides in your reply merely to agree with a board member

Frequently, a member will take a contrary position merely to draw you out and to see if you are willing and able to defend your point of view. Do not start a debate, yet do not surrender a good position. If a position is worth taking, it is worth defending.

14) Do not be afraid to admit an error in judgment if you are shown to be wrong

The board knows that you are forced to reply without any opportunity for careful consideration. Your answer may be demonstrably wrong. If so, admit it and get on with the interview.

15) Do not dwell at length on your present job

The opening question may relate to your present assignment. Answer the question but do not go into an extended discussion. You are being examined for a *new* job, not your present one. As a matter of fact, try to phrase ALL your answers in terms of the job for which you are being examined.

Basis of Rating

Probably you will forget most of these "do's" and "don'ts" when you walk into the oral interview room. Even remembering them all will not ensure you a passing grade. Perhaps you did not have the qualifications in the first place. But remembering them will help you to put your best foot forward, without treading on the toes of the board members.

Rumor and popular opinion to the contrary notwithstanding, an oral board wants you to make the best appearance possible. They know you are under pressure – but they also want to see how you respond to it as a guide to what your reaction would be under the pressures of the job you seek. They will be influenced by the degree of poise you display, the personal traits you show and the manner in which you respond.

EXAMINATION SECTION

EXAMINATION SECTION
TEST 1

DIRECTIONS: Each question or incomplete statement is followed by several suggested answers or completions. Select the one that BEST answers the question or completes the statement. *PRINT THE LETTER OF THE CORRECT ANSWER IN THE SPACE AT THE RIGHT.*

1. The MOST efficient devices to measure the gaseous pollutant content of an air sample are   1._____

    A. cyclones   B. filters
    C. bubblers   D. settling chambers

2. The source MOST likely to cause high concentrations of toxic metals associated with nonpoint source water pollution is   2._____

    A. construction   B. highway de-icing
    C. on-site sewage disposal   D. urban storm runoff

3. In the United States, the required landfill space per person each year is GENERALLY   3._____

    A. ten cubic feet   B. one cubic yard
    C. one cubic acre   D. ten square feet

4. The easiest and most effective method for controlling air pollution is   4._____

    A. source correction   B. treatment
    C. collection   D. dispersion

5. The MOST serious source of air pollution associated with the automobile is the   5._____

    A. fuel tank   B. carburetor
    C. crankcase   D. exhaust

6. Which of the following practices or devices is considered to be a collection or treatment control for urban storm-water runoff?   6._____

    A. Anti-littering laws   B. Street cleaning
    C. Floodplain zoning   D. Detention systems

7. The increasing trend in solid waste disposal in the United States is toward the practice of   7._____

    A. incineration
    B. ocean dumping
    C. sanitary landfill
    D. recycling/resource reclamation

8. The MOST widely practiced method for cooling air pollutants before they reach control equipment is   8._____

    A. dilution   B. settling
    C. heat exchange coils   D. quenching

9. Which of the following is NOT a factor of required knowledge for solving an upgrade problem in wastewater treatment plants?   9._____

A. Staffing pattern
B. Normal operational and maintenance procedures
C. Daily peak flow rates
D. Condition of process hardware

10. The category of solid waste that constitutes the GREATEST volume percentage in the United States is   10._

    A. residential   B. bulky wastes
    C. commercial   D. industrial

11. In current practice, the SIMPLEST test for ozone content of an air sample measures the air's reaction with   11._

    A. metals with high lead content
    B. rubber
    C. organics
    D. copper

12. High concentrations of acid pollutants associated with nonpoint source water pollution are MOST likely to be contributed by   12._

    A. non-coal mining   B. air pollution fallout
    C. agriculture   D. forestry

13. Which of the following methods is used by analysts to measure the concentration of hydrocarbons in an air supply?   13._

    A. Chemical luminescence   B. Flame ionization
    C. Infrared spectrometry   D. High-volume sampling

14. Environmental engineers generally consider _____ to be the BEST cover material for sanitary landfill sites.   14._

    A. sandy loam   B. clay
    C. gravel   D. silt

15. Deceleration of an automobile is most likely to cause the HIGHEST relative increase in the amount of   15._

    A. hydrocarbons   B. carbon monoxide
    C. nitrogen oxides   D. lead

16. The _____ method for sanitary landfilling involves the distribution of waste into discrete cells.   16._

    A. slope   B. area   C. ramp   D. trench

17. A DISADVANTAGE associated with the use of controlled burning for solid waste disposal is   17._

    A. consumption of a large amount of resources
    B. lingering contamination of burn site
    C. increased transport costs
    D. large land area required

18. Each of the following is a primary factor in the determination of the area required for a sanitary landfill site EXCEPT   18.____

   A.   percent reduction, by compaction, of on-site refuse volume
   B.   amount of cover material required
   C.   total projected amount of refuse to be delivered
   D.   average density of refuse delivered to landfill

19. The method of solid waste disposal that currently involves the GREATEST costs in capital investment is   19.____

   A.   incineration   B.   ocean dumping
   C.   landfilling   D.   composting

20. The substance normally used in filters to detect the presence of sulfur dioxide in an air sample is   20.____

   A.   microorganisms   B.   sulfur
   C.   lead peroxide   D.   carbon

21. Which of the following is NOT a quality parameter of concern in the activated carbon treatment of wastewater?   21.____

   A.   Heavy metals   B.   Suspended solids
   C.   Trace organics   D.   Dissolved oxygen

22. The problem that presents the GREATEST potential hazard to landfill sites is   22.____

   A.   pests   B.   water pollution
   C.   gas   D.   decomposition

23. The MOST serious problem associated with the investigative practice of industrial stack sampling is   23.____

   A.   control of potentially great capital expense
   B.   risk of obtaining an unrepresentative sample
   C.   safety risks for analysts
   D.   skewing of sample readings by heat concentrations

24. The MOST common method for disinfection in wastewater treatment plants is   24.____

   A.   ozone treatment
   B.   ultraviolet light exposure
   C.   chlorination
   D.   introduction of bromine chloride

25. Of the following categories for the pollution control of urban stormwater runoff, _____ controls are considered to be the MOST effective and inexpensive.   25.____

   A.   planning   B.   accumulation
   C.   treatment   D.   collection

KEY (CORRECT ANSWERS)

1.	C		11.	B
2.	D		12.	A
3.	B		13.	B
4.	A		14.	A
5.	D		15.	A
6.	D		16.	B
7.	D		17.	C
8.	C		18.	C
9.	C		19.	D
10.	D		20.	C

21. A
22. B
23. B
24. C
25. A

TEST 2

DIRECTIONS: Each question or incomplete statement is followed by several suggested answers or completions. Select the one that BEST answers the question or completes the statement. *PRINT THE LETTER OF THE CORRECT ANSWER IN THE SPACE AT THE RIGHT.*

1. _____% of solid waste in the United States is considered compostible.　　　1._____

   A. 5-10　　　　　B. 20-30　　　　　C. 50-75　　　　　D. 80-85

2. Which of the following is NOT considered to be a factor affecting the level of organic　　2._____
decomposition in sanitary landfills?

   A. Moisture　　　　　　　　　B. Surface area of fill
   C. Temperature　　　　　　　　D. Depth of fill

3. The SIMPLEST and MOST widely used device for controlling the particulate content of　　3._____
an air supply is the

   A. settling chamber　　　　　　B. adsorber
   C. wet collector　　　　　　　　D. bubbler

4. The agricultural practice MOST likely to contribute high levels of total dissolved solids to　　4._____
nonpoint source water pollution is

   A. animal production
   B. irrigated crop production
   C. pasturing and rangeland
   D. non-irrigated crop production

5. Pathogenic bacteria in wastewater supplies are likely to be produced by each of the fol-　　5._____
lowing EXCEPT

   A. construction operations
   B. food processing industries
   C. pharmaceutical manufacturing
   D. tanneries

6. The substance MOST often used to remove sulfur from discharged flue gases is　　6._____

   A. copper　　　　　B. lime　　　　　C. water　　　　　D. acid

7. In controlling automotive emissions, an activated carbon canister is used to store emis-　　7._____
sions from the

   A. manifold　　　　　　　　　B. fuel tank
   C. crankcase　　　　　　　　　D. exhaust

8. Which of the following is NOT a disadvantage associated with the use of sanitary landfill　　8._____
sites for solid waste disposal?

   A. High collection costs
   B. Jurisdiction entanglements
   C. Large amount of land required
   D. Difficulties presented by seasonal changes

9. The Ringelmann scale is a device used to measure the _____ of an air sample.   9.

    A. smoke density   B. odor
    C. temperature   D. gaseous pollutant content

10. High-volume sampling is a method for detecting   10.

    A. ozone   B. oxidant
    C. particulate   D. sulfur dioxide

11. An example of air pollution abatement, as opposed to source control, is   11.

    A. change of raw material   B. modification of process
    C. equipment modifications   D. stack dispersion

12. *Pollutant loading* is a term that defines the   12.

    A. collection of pollutants for treatment in a control exercise
    B. quantity of pollution detached and transported into surface watercourses
    C. saturation point of any environment in terms of its pollutant capacity
    D. process of contamination, by an industrial source, of the ambient air

13. Each of the following is an advantage associated with the controlled burning of solid   13.
wastes EXCEPT

    A. land can be returned to immediate use
    B. sites are longer-lasting
    C. reduced amount of required land
    D. relatively easy collection and transport of materials

14. The device capable of removing the smallest particle from an air supply is the   14

    A. electrostatic precipitator
    B. settling chamber
    C. bag filter
    D. wet collector

15. High concentrations of suspended solids associated with nonpoint source water pollution   15
are MOST likely contributed by

    A. urban storm runoff
    B. construction
    C. air pollution fallout
    D. non-irrigated crop production

16. Which of the following is NOT one of the primary steps involved in the control of gaseous   16
air pollutants?

    A. Removal of pollutant from emissions
    B. Change in process producing pollutant
    C. Dispersion of the pollutant
    D. Chemical conversion of the pollutant

17. To control automotive air pollution, the process of recycling blow-by gases is a method   17._____
for controlling emissions from the

    A. fuel tank
    B. exhaust
    C. carburetor
    D. crankcase

18. In testing a water supply for the presence of coliform bacteria, the survey method MOST   18._____
likely to be used is

    A. oxygen demand
    B. dissolved oxygen
    C. total dissolved solids
    D. suspended solids

19. In measuring the constituency of a given air supply, analysts use the process of infrared   19._____
spectrometry to determine concentrations of

    A. oxidants
    B. carbon monoxide
    C. sulfur dioxide
    D. particulates

20. Which of the following is NOT one of the primary factors affecting the choice of pollution   20._____
control methods for urban stormwater runoff?

    A. Specific constituents of runoff
    B. Type of sewage system
    C. Status of area development
    D. Method of land use

21. A disadvantage associated with the use of sanitary landfill sites for solid waste disposal   21._____
is

    A. high personnel and plant costs
    B. weakened accomodation of peak quantities
    C. potential for groundwater pollution
    D. difficulty with unusual, bulky materials

22. The MOST serious problem in air pollution is presented by   22._____

    A. cooling of pollutants
    B. treatment of pollutants
    C. collection of pollutants
    D. source modifications

23. Of the following practices or devices, the one considered to be an accumulation control   23._____
for urban stormwater runoff is

    A. automobile inspection
    B. street cleaning
    C. floodplain zoning
    D. catch basins

24. _____ is used to survey an air sample for the presence of sulfur dioxide.   24._____

    A. Liquid medium
    B. Colorimetry
    C. High-volume sampling
    D. Flame ionization

25. Acceleration of an automobile is most likely to cause the HIGHEST relative increase in   25._____
the amount of

    A. hydrocarbons
    B. carbon monoxide
    C. nitrogen oxides
    D. lead

KEY (CORRECT ANSWERS)

1.	D	11.	D
2.	B	12.	B
3.	A	13.	D
4.	B	14.	A
5.	A	15.	B
6.	B	16.	C
7.	B	17.	D
8.	A	18.	A
9.	A	19.	B
10.	C	20.	A

21.	C
22.	C
23.	B
24.	B
25.	C

———

EXAMINATION SECTION
TEST 1

DIRECTIONS: Each question or incomplete statement is followed by several suggested answers or completions. Select the one that BEST answers the question or completes the statement. *PRINT THE LETTER OF THE CORRECT ANSWER IN THE SPACE AT THE RIGHT.*

1. The slope characteristic necessary to classify a soil quantity as having only slight limitations for development as an area landfill site is _____%.
   A. 0   B. 0-8   C. 0-15   D. over 8   1.____

2. On average, the amount of municipal refuse produced by a single person in one day is APPROXIMATELY _____ pounds.
   A. 1.5-2.5   B. 2.0-3.5   C. 3.5-5.5   D. 4-6.5   2.____

3. The percentage of solid waste in the United States directly disposed of on land is APPROXIMATELY _____%.
   A. 40   B. 55   C. 70   D. 85   3.____

4. What device is used for the monitoring and study of landfill leachate?
   A. Precipitator   B. Deglasser
   C. Lysimeter   D. Manometer   4.____

5. Which stage in the approval of a landfill site would occur LAST?
   A. Hearing   B. Appeals
   C. Site selection   D. Study   5.____

6. Site development plans for a sanitary landfill should include initial and final topography at a contour interval of _____ meter(s) or _____.
   A. 1; more   B. 1.5; less
   C. 2; more   D. 2.5; less   6.____

7. Which piece of landfill equipment or machinery is MOST effective for spreading solid waste?
   A. Crawler loader   B. Dragline
   C. Rubber-tired loader   D. Crawler dozer   7.____

8. The cover material BEST suited for keeping burrowing animals from penetrating a landfill site is
   A. clay   B. gravel
   C. clean sand   D. silty sand   8.____

9. The recommended number of equipment operators for use at a landfill site handling 500 tons of waste per day is
   A. 1   B. 2   C. 6   D. 12   9.____

10. What accounts for the GREATEST portion of a sanitary landfill's operating costs?
    A. Administration   B. Equipment
    C. Overhead   D. Wages

10._

11. In a typical sanitary landfill leachate quantity, _____ is found to be in the HIGHEST concentration.
    A. chloride   B. lead   C. sodium   D. zinc

11._

12. Under normal conditions, _____ miles is considered to be economical for collection vehicles that deliver solid waste to a landfill site.
    A. 5-15   B. 15-30   C. 25-40   D. 30-50

12._

13. In order to be classified as *high density*, baled solid waste must be baled to _____ pounds per cubic foot.
    A. 40-60   B. 50-60   C. 60-70   D. 75-90

13._

14. Clay liners are used in many landfill sites to prevent or *attenuate* the seepage of chemicals and organic material. For which of the following substances would a clay liner be rated as having *moderate* attenuation qualities?
    A. Mercury   B. Lead   C. Iron   D. Calcium

14._

15. Groundwater monitoring systems used at a landfill site typically include AT LEAST _____ monitoring well(s) down-gradient from the site.
    A. 1   B. 1-2   C. 2-3   D. 2-5

15._

16. The LEAST effective method for the treatment of strong landfill leachates is
    A. rotating biological contractors
    B. anaerobic digesters
    C. trickling filters
    D. aerated lagoons

16._

17. The MOST effective device for monitoring and analyzing landfill gases is a
    A. lysimeter   B. dry well
    C. steel probe   D. gas chromatograph

17._

18. In order to classify a soil quantity as having only slight limitations for development as a trench landfill site, _____ inches of soil above hard bedrock is necessary.
    A. 36-48   B. 48-60
    C. 60-72   D. more than 72

18._

19. The common landfill practice for disposal of bulky wastes such as car bodies is to
    A. dig a hole in the working face in order to backfill the heavier wastes
    B. place them on the surface of the working face, at the bottom

19._

C. place them on the surface of the working face, in the middle

D. spread them evenly over the top of the landfill site, just before applying cover material

20. Which ionic substance is MOST commonly used as a tracer for tracking landfill leachate influence on an area's groundwater supply?
    A. Nitrogen   B. Chloride   C. Sodium   D. Sulfide   20.___

21. Under normal conditions, baled waste can be expected to *rebound*, or re-expand, to an extent of _____%.   21.___
    A. 5-10   B. 10-15   C. 20-30   D. 35-50

22. Under normal conditions, _____ cubic yards of landfill space are needed to meet the annual needs of a municipal population of approximately 10,000.   22.___
    A. 4,000-16,000   B. 12,000-26,000
    C. 16,000-32,000   D. 24,000-48,000

23. Until conditions have been found to be satisfactory for two consecutive inspections at a new or probationary landfill site, federal regulations require a state or local inspection   23.___
    A. semi-monthly   B. monthly
    C. every six months   D. annually

24. A crawler dozer at a landfill site can be used economically for moving earth or waste over distances of up to   24.___
    A. 100 feet   B. 300 feet
    C. one-fourth of a mile   D. one mile

25. When spreading solid waste into layers at a landfill site, each layer should be no more than _____ feet deep.   25.___
    A. 2   B. 4   C. 6   D. 12

KEY (CORRECT ANSWERS)

1. B		11. A	
2. C		12. C	
3. D		13. C	
4. C		14. C	
5. B		15. C	
6. B		16. C	
7. D		17. D	
8. B		18. D	
9. B		19. B	
10. D		20. B	
	21. B		
	22. C		
	23. B		
	24. B		
	25. A		

TEST 2

DIRECTIONS: Each question or incomplete statement is followed by several suggested answers or completions. Select the one that BEST answers the question or completes the statement. *PRINT THE LETTER OF THE CORRECT ANSWER IN THE SPACE AT THE RIGHT.*

1. The MOST expensive material for use as a sanitary landfill liner is
   A. butyl rubber
   B. Hypalon
   C. chlorinated polyethylene
   D. polyvinyl chloride

   1.__

2. The depth of cover material recommended for an area in which new cells will NOT be added for at least 30 days is
   A. 1 inch   B. 6 inches   C. 1 foot   D. 2 feet

   2.__

3. What is the term for the two-piece hydraulic bucket used on loaders at a landfill site?
   A. Grapple
   B. Bullclam
   C. Grouser
   D. U-blade

   3.__

4. MOST rubber-tired equipment used at landfill sites can be operated economically at distances of up to
   A. 300 feet
   B. 600 feet
   C. half a mile
   D. one mile

   4.__

5. The percentage of a landfill's total operating expenses consumed by the cost of monitoring operations is ____%.
   A. 0-1   B. 2-5   C. 5-8   D. 8-12

   5.__

6. The BEST possible soil type for excavating and working a trench landfill site is
   A. silty sand
   B. clay
   C. sandy loam
   D. clayey-silty sand

   6.__

7. What type of landfill equipment or machinery is MOST effective for use in large excavation operations?
   A. Landfill compactor
   B. Dragline
   C. Rubber-tired loader
   D. Scraper

   7.__

8. Clay landfill liners have proven virtually incapable of seepage prevention of
   A. mercury   B. zinc   C. potassium   D. calcium

   8.__

9. The typical moisture content of mixed municipal solid waste is ____%.
   A. 3-5   B. 10-18   C. 20-30   D. 25-40

   9.__

10. What permeability rate, in inches per hour, is the MINIMUM necessary in order to classify a soil quantity as having only slight limitations for development as an area landfill site?
    A. 1   B. 2   C. 3   D. 4

    10.__

11. The MAXIMUM waste cell density, in pounds per cubic yard, that can be achieved through *moderate* compacting efforts is

    A. 500   B. 800   C. 1000   D. 1500

11.____

12. The MAXIMUM haul capacity, in pounds per cubic yard, for most scrapers used at a landfill site is

    A. 2   B. 12   C. 28   D. 40

12.____

13. What type of landfill equipment or machinery is MOST effective for spreading cover material over a landfill cell or site?

    A. Rubber-tired loader   B. Crawler dozer
    C. Dragline   D. Landfill compactor

13.____

14. The term for the vertical distance of a compacted volume of solid waste plus the thickness of the waste's cover material is called

    A. cell depth   B. cell thickness
    C. trench height   D. lift depth

14.____

15. When using a dragline during trench landfill operations, the guideline for the dragline's boom length is _____ the trench _____.

    A. half; depth   B. twice; depth
    C. half; width   D. twice; width

15.____

16. After a landfill's final cover has been graded to the desired level, stakes with _____ tops are planted on the surface to signal completion.

    A. green   B. red   C. orange   D. blue

16.____

17. Industry standards require that no solid waste, regardless of its type, should be exposed for a period of more than

    A. 6 hours   B. 12 hours   C. 24 hours   D. two days

17.____

18. The cover material BEST suited for the growing of vegetation over a completed landfill site is

    A. silt   B. clayey-silty sand
    C. clean sand   D. clay

18.____

19. Which of the following landfill vehicles is the quickest and most mobile during operation?

    A. Rubber-tired loader   B. Dozer
    C. Landfill compactor   D. Dragline

19.____

20. The problem of gas migration within a landfill can be solved by either active or passive methods.
Which of the following statements about passive gas migration control is FALSE?
It

    A. is limited to shallow sites
    B. involves the installation of venting trenches backfilled with stone

20.____

C. uses natural vacuums to control gases
D. is typically employed beyond the landfill boundary

21. The MINIMUM recommended density, in pounds per cubic
    yard (lb/yd^3), for compacted waste cells in a sanitary
    landfill is
       A. 500   B. 800   C. 1000   D. 1500
          21.__

22. The GREATEST danger to people at or near a sanitary
    landfill site is from
       A. equipment failure   B. gas production
       C. dioxin poisoning   D. organic water pollution
          22.__

23. Which organic waste's decomposition generates the GREATEST
    amount of gas within a landfill?
       A. Protein   B. Cellulose
       C. Carbohydrate   D. Fat
          23.__

24. The impermeable liner that is placed below the base of a
    landfill site to prevent seepage is USUALLY _____ in
    thickness.
       A. 6-12 inches   B. 12-28 inches
       C. 1-3 feet   D. 2-6 feet
          24.__

25. According to industry recommendations, the MINIMUM number
    of personnel used to operate a landfill site should be
       A. 2   B. 3   C. 4   D. 5
          25.__

KEY (CORRECT ANSWERS)

1. A		11. C
2. C		12. D
3. B		13. B
4. B		14. D
5. B		15. D
6. B		16. D
7. B		17. B
8. D		18. B
9. C		19. A
10. B		20. C

21. B
22. B
23. D
24. C
25. A

EXAMINATION SECTION
TEST 1

DIRECTIONS: Each question or incomplete statement is followed by several suggested answers or completions. Select the one that BEST answers the question or completes the statement. *PRINT THE LETTER OF THE CORRECT ANSWER IN THE SPACE AT THE RIGHT.*

Questions 1-20.

DIRECTIONS: Questions 1 through 20 are to be answered SOLELY on the basis of the information contained in the following passage, the CREW CHIEF'S REPORT, and the HEALTH INSPECTOR'S REPORT.

Block 421 is located in a heavily industrialized part of the city. There are eight six-story apartment buildings on the block. Each of these apartment buildings contains 24 five-room apartments.

When a child living in one of the apartment buildings on block 421 needs medical care, he is taken to the privately-owned child clinic a few blocks away. Dr. Stone, the director of the clinic, recently learned that 25 of the 40 children treated by his clinic for rat bites within the past year lived on block 421 at the time they were bitten. He was so concerned about the conditions on that block that he wrote a letter to the Department of Health requesting that a pest control team be sent there to help reduce the rodent threat to children living on block 421.

In response to Dr. Stone's letter, a team of 20 pest control workers under the supervision of a crew chief named John Angelo was sent to work on block 421. They remained there for a period of four weeks. During the first week, the pest control workers cleared the garbage from the streets and backyards of the block while the crew chief inspected all of the apartment buildings there to determine the extent of the rodent infestation. The crew chief and his staff spent the second week cleaning up the basements, halls, and stairs of each apartment building on the block and filling in whatever rat holes they found there. During the third week, they placed rat poison in the basements and apartments of each building. They spent the fourth week instructing the tenants of block 421 on how to keep their apartments clean of rats. Just before they left the block for the last time, Mr. Angelo placed a sign in the lobby of each apartment house which gave the name, address, and telephone number of the director of the nearest rodent control office. All of the tenants were urged to phone this number if the problem with rodents developed again.

After three months had passed and nobody from block 421 called the rodent control office to complain of a rat problem, the health department concluded that rodents were no longer a problem on block 421 and they concentrated their efforts elsewhere. Then they received a letter from Dr. Stone which said that children living on block 421 were coming to the clinic with rat bites again. He demanded that the health department conduct a follow-up inspection to determine just how successful they had been in removing rats from the block.

In response to Dr. Stone's second letter, a health inspector named Harry Rosen was sent to block 421 to make a follow-up inspection. He discovered that the block showed as many signs of rodent infestation as it had when the pest control team had first inspected the block, prior to cleaning it up. Mr. Rosen recommended that a second pest control team be sent to block 421 and that a more intensive community education program be conducted after the block was once again cleaned up and the rodents were once again removed.

Reports were prepared by both the crew chief and the health inspector concerning their inspection of block 421. Copies of each of these reports labeled the CREW CHIEF'S REPORT and the HEALTH INSPECTOR'S REPORT follow.

CREW CHIEF'S REPORT

DATE INSPECTION COMPLETED: August 17, 19   PREPARED BY: John Angelo, Crew Chief
BLOCK INSPECTED: 421

Bldg. Address	No. of Apts. Needing Exterminating	Conditions Found in Public Areas	Conditions Found in Apartments
5 Pier St.	12	Halls and stairs badly littered. Rat burrows in backyard.	Kitchen floors food stained. Rat holes in baseboards.
11 Pier St.	7	Basement entrance blocked by debris. Rat droppings in basement.	Uncovered garbage in kitchens. Garbage frequently thrown out windows.
6 Water Rd.	20	Holes in basement floors need filling. Rat holes behind boiler.	Rat droppings in foyers. Uncovered garbage in kitchens.
10 Water Rd.	14	Rat droppings in basement. Dead rats spotted in basement.	Kitchen floors food stained. Rat holes in baseboards.
5 Bay Rd.	4	Fire escapes littered. Backyard filled with sewage due to backup.	Garbage frequently thrown out windows. Uncovered garbage in kitchens.
9 Bay Rd.	24	Basement entrance blocked by debris. Rat holes behind boiler.	Uncovered food containers on counters. Kitchen floors food stained.
10 Canal St.	10	Rat droppings in basement. Halls and stairs badly littered.	Rat holes in baseboards. Uncovered garbage in kitchens.
14 Canal St.	14	Rat tracks seen in backyard. Basement entrance blocked by debris.	Rat holes in baseboards. Uncovered food containers on counters.

HEALTH INSPECTOR'S REPORT

DATE INSPECTION COMPLETED: April 17,   PREPARED BY: Harry Rosen, Health Inspector

BLOCK INSPECTED: 421

Bldg. Address	No. of Apts. Needing Exterminating	Conditions Found in Public Areas	Conditions Found in Apartments
5 Pier St.	8	Rat droppings in basement. Basement entrance blocked by debris.	Rat holes in baseboards. Uncovered garbage in kitchens.
11 Pier St.	12	Rat holes behind boiler. Holes in basement floor need filling.	Rat holes in baseboards. Kitchen floors food stained.
6 Water Rd.	24	Rat holes behind boiler. Halls and stairs badly littered.	Holes in kitchen walls behind sink. Rat holes in baseboards.
10 Water Rd.	14	Basement entrance blocked by debris. Traces of old rat bait found in cellar.	Garbage frequently thrown out windows. Uncovered garbage in kitchens.
5 Bay Rd.	6	Rat droppings in basement. Dead rats found in basement.	Holes in kitchen walls behind sink. Rat droppings in foyers.
9 Bay Rd.	17	Basement entrance blocked by debris. Fire escapes littered.	Rat holes in baseboards. Uncovered food containers on counters.
10 Canal St.	14	Entrance to building badly littered. Rat holes behind boiler.	Kitchen floors food stained. Uncovered garbage in kitchens.
14 Canal St.	21	Rat droppings in basement. Halls and stairs badly littered.	Garbage frequently thrown out windows. Rat holes in baseboards.

1. The total number of apartments on block 421 is   1.___
   A. 144   B. 192   C. 960   D. 1152

2. When children living on block 421 need health care, they   2.___
   are taken to the
   A. child clinic   B. family doctor
   C. Health Department   D. hospital

3. Pest control workers were sent to block 421 because   3.___
   A. the block is in a highly industrialized part of the
      city
   B. numerous tenants complained of rodent infestation on
      the block
   C. Dr. Stone asked that they be sent there
   D. forty children living on that block had been bitten
      by rats

4. The pest control workers left block 421 after they had   4.___
   been working there for _____ week(s).
   A. one   B. two   C. three   D. four

5. An inspection of the buildings on block 421 was INITIALLY 5.___
   made by
   A. Dr. Stone   B. a pest control worker
   C. Harry Rosen   D. John Angelo

6. In treating the rodent-infested buildings on block 421,   6.___
   the pest control workers placed rat poison
   A. in basements and apartments
   B. in building lobbies
   C. in halls and on stairs
   D. on streets and in backyards

7. Just before they left block 421, the pest control workers 7.___
   A. cleared the buildings and surrounding areas of
      garbage
   B. placed rat bait wherever it was needed
   C. placed a sign in the lobby of each building
   D. told the tenants how they could keep their apartments
      clean

8. After the pest control team finished its job, the Health   8.___
   Department thought that block 421 was clean of rodents
   because
   A. they had received no further complaints from Dr. Stone
   B. they had received no complaints from the tenants who
      lived there
   C. no more children on the block were being bitten by
      rodents
   D. a follow-up inspection had found no further evidence
      of rodents there

9. When a health inspector from the Department of Health   9.___
    conducted a follow-up inspection of block 421, he learned
    that
        A. the block was still rat infested
        B. the block was now free of rodents
        C. all of the buildings now had their own exterminators
        D. some of the buildings had been abandoned

10. The health inspector who conducted the follow-up inspec-   10.___
    tion recommended that
        A. the building owners hire their own exterminators
        B. a second pest control team be sent to work on block
           421
        C. block 421 needed no further pest control work
        D. all of the buildings on block 421 be demolished

11. The health inspector found the largest number of apart-   11.___
    ments needing exterminating in the building at
        A. 6 Water Road   B. 10 Water Road
        C. 9 Bay Road   D. 14 Canal Street

12. In which of the following buildings did the crew chief   12.___
    find the fewest number of apartments needing exterminat-
    ing?
        A. 5 Pier Street   B. 11 Pier Street
        C. 9 Bay Road   D. 10 Canal Street

13. In which of the following buildings did Harry Rosen find   13.___
    food stained kitchen floors?
        A. 5 Pier Street   B. 6 Water Road
        C. 9 Bay Road   D. 10 Canal Street

14. In which of the following buildings did John Angelo find   14.___
    the basement entrance blocked by debris?
        A. 5 Pier Street   B. 10 Water Road
        C. 9 Bay Road   D. 10 Canal Street

15. In which of the following buildings did the health inspec-   15.___
    tor find littered fire escapes?
        A. 11 Pier Street   B. 6 Water Road
        C. 5 Bay Road   D. 9 Bay Road

16. Harry Rosen found rat holes in the baseboards of apart-   16.___
    ments in all of the following buildings EXCEPT
        A. 5 Pier Street   B. 10 Water Road
        C. 9 Bay Road   D. 14 Canal Street

17. How much time passed between the time the crew chief   17.___
    completed his inspection and the time the health inspec-
    tor completed his?
        A. 4 weeks   B. 4 months   C. 6 months   D. 8 months

18. The only building in which both Harry Rosen and John   18.___
    Angelo found 14 apartments needing extermination was
       A. 11 Pier Street   B. 10 Water Road
       C. 10 Canal Street   D. 14 Canal Street

19. The total number of apartments which the crew chief found   19.___
    in need of exterminating was
       A. 76   B. 87   C. 105   D. 116

20. The building in which Harry Rosen found 12 apartments   20.___
    needing exterminating was
       A. 5 Pier Street   B. 11 Pier Street
       C. 6 Water Road   D. 14 Canal Street

———

KEY (CORRECT ANSWERS)

1. B		11. A
2. A		12. B
3. C		13. D
4. D		14. C
5. D		15. D
6. A		16. B
7. C		17. D
8. B		18. B
9. A		19. C
10. B		20. B

———

TEST 2

DIRECTIONS: Each question or incomplete statement is followed by several suggested answers or completions. Select the one that BEST answers the question or completes the statement. *PRINT THE LETTER OF THE CORRECT ANSWER IN THE SPACE AT THE RIGHT.*

Questions 1-10.

DIRECTIONS: Questions 1 through 10 are to be answered SOLELY on the basis of the information contained in the following passage and refer to entries that would be made on the FIELD VISIT REPORT form that follows the passage.

On March 6, a crew composed of five Community Service Aides and three Pest Control Aides, under the supervision of a Crew Chief (Pest Control), made a field visit to inspect several residential buildings and a vacant lot. The purpose of the visit was to check for exposed refuse and signs of rats, mice, and insects. If conditions needed correction, they were to recommend the actions that should be taken.

The crew was driven in a department car to the first inspection site, an apartment house at 124 Grand Street, arriving at 11:30 A.M. When the crew members inspected the apartment house, they discovered rats and holes in the baseboards in several of the apartments. The landlord had not placed enough bait boxes in the basement. The Crew Chief recommended that an exterminator be scheduled to treat the building. The crew left the building at 12:05 P.M. and walked to the next inspection site at 129 Grand Street.

The crew arrived at the second site at 12:10 P.M. and left at 12:40 P.M. Because the crew found rats and roaches in the building, the Crew Chief immediately called the office and made arrangements for an exterminator to treat the building that afternoon. The Crew Chief recommended that the building should be re-inspected the following week to see if the exterminating had been successful.

The crew workers walked to the next inspection site, a vacant lot on Lucke Street, across the street from an apartment building at 350 Lucke Street. They observed that refuse covered much of the area of the vacant lot. The Crew Chief recommended that a clean-up team be scheduled to remove refuse from the lot.

The crew's last inspection of the day was a building at 300 Lucke Street. They walked to this site, arrived at 1:00 P.M., and stayed for an hour. They inspected several apartments in the building to see if a recent extermination had been successful. Upon seeing that no further work was needed at the site, they returned to their office by subway.

The Crew Chief arrived at the office at 3:00 P.M. and made out the following FIELD VISIT REPORT form:

FIELD VISIT REPORT FORM

1. Date_____

2. Time Arrived at First Site_____

3. Purpose of Field Visit_____
_____
_____

4. Number of Persons in Crew (Not including Crew Chief (Pest Control)_____
_____

5. Transportation_____

6. Number of Sites Visited_____

7. Addresses of Sites Visited_____
_____
_____
_____

8. Conditions Noted_____
_____
_____
_____

9. Recommendations_____
_____
_____
_____

10. Arrangements Made by Crew Chief While in the Field
_____
_____
_____

11. Time Left Last Site_____

1. Which of the following should be entered on line 2?   1.___
   A. 11:30 A.M.   B. 12:05 P.M.
   C. 12:10 P.M.   D. 12:40 P.M.

2. Which of the following should be entered on line 3?   2.___
   A. Exterminate apartment buildings that have rats and mice
   B. Examine various sites for exposed refuse and signs of
      rats, mice, and insects
   C. Inspect work done by clean-up team
   D. Clean up lots that are covered with refuse

3. The number that should be entered on line 4 is   3.___
   A. 3   B. 5   C. 8   D. 9

4. Which of the following should be entered on line 6?   4.___
   A. 3   B. 4   C. 5   D. 6

5. Each of the following should be entered on line 7 EXCEPT   5.___
   A. 124 Grand Street   B. 129 Grand Street
   C. 300 Lucke Street   D. 350 Lucke Street

6. Each of the following should be entered on line 8 EXCEPT   6.___
   the presence of
   A. holes in the baseboards at 124 Grand Street
   B. insects, rats, and mice at 300 Lucke Street
   C. refuse at the vacant lot on Lucke Street
   D. rats and roaches at 129 Grand Street

7. Which of the following should be entered on line 5?   7.___
   A. Department car to first site, subway between sites
   B. Subway to first site, walked between sites
   C. Walked to first site, department car between sites
   D. Department car to first site, walked between sites

8. All of the following should be entered on line 9 EXCEPT: 8.___
   A. Extermination at 124 Grand Street to remove rats
   B. Clean-up at the lot on Lucke Street to remove refuse
   C. Follow-up visit at 129 Grand Street to determine
      success of extermination
   D. Clean-up building at 300 Lucke Street to end infes-
      tation

9. Which of the following should be entered on line 10?   9.___
   A. Extermination of building at 129 Grand Street
   B. Extermination of building at 124 Grand Street
   C. Clean-up of lot on Lucke Street
   D. Clean-up of building at 300 Lucke Street

10. Which of the following should be entered on line 11?   10.___
   _____ P.M.
   A. 12:40   B. 1:00   C. 2:00   D. 3:00

KEY (CORRECT ANSWERS)

1. A	6. B
2. B	7. D
3. C	8. D
4. B	9. A
5. D	10. C

EXAMINATION SECTION
TEST 1

DIRECTIONS: Each question or incomplete statement is followed by several suggested answers or completions. Select the one that BEST answers the question or completes the statement. *PRINT THE LETTER OF THE CORRECT ANSWER IN THE SPACE AT THE RIGHT.*

1. When a snowfall predicted to be heavy begins, you should schedule the spreaders to operate _____ the snowfall.   1.___
   A. only at the beginning of
   B. only at the end of
   C. during the entire duration of
   D. at hourly intervals throughout

2. One common method of dealing with snow accumulation on streets is *scattering*.   2.___
   Scattering refers to
   A. spreading salt into traffic lanes
   B. plowing snow into traffic lanes
   C. sprinkling ashes into traffic lanes
   D. pushing snow onto little-used sidewalks

3. The department may hire private contractors to provide equipment and personnel to assist in snow removal.   3.___
   The one of the following factors which helps to determine the number of work gangs that a contractor should supply for snow removal work in a contract area is the
   A. contractor's opinion of what is necessary to provide the required service
   B. previous measurements of the amount of snowfall in the area
   C. number of sanitation trucks available
   D. number and character of the regular sanitation districts in the snow removal area

4. The MAIN reason for the establishment of weather condition stations by the department is to provide weather information during   4.___
   A. rainy periods   B. dry spells
   C. hurricane season   D. snow season

5. A reason why hydrants are NOT used in flushing operations when temperatures are 34°F or lower is that the   5.___
   A. water pressure in the hydrants may be too low
   B. hydrants may be more difficult to open
   C. water from the hydrants may freeze on the streets
   D. water may not flow out of the hydrants fast enough

6. The *only* instance in which sewer manholes may be opened   6.__
   and used by the sanitation department is for
   A. disposal of snow during snow season
   B. removal of leaves in the fall
   C. drainage of streets during heavy rains
   D. disposal of confetti after parades

7. The purpose of dirt deflectors on a mechanical broom is to   7.__
   A. prevent dust and dirt from being swept beyond the
      path of the pick-up broom
   B. scrape dust and dirt off the gutter broom to keep it
      from becoming clogged
   C. prevent dust and dirt from fouling the shaft of the
      gutter brooms
   D. guide the swept-up dirt and dust from the conveyor
      to the hopper

8. A driver has been assigned to operate a Wayne mechanical   8.__
   broom to sweep a street on which there is much heavily-
   packed debris.
   The one of the following which is the MOST proper speed
   and gear range that the driver should use when sweeping
   this heavily-packed debris is _____ miles an hour in
   _____ gear.
   A. two; first   B. five; second
   C. eight; third   D. fifteen; fourth

9. Of the following pieces of motorized cleaning and collec-   9.__
   tion equipment, the one that would be MOST proper to use
   for areas not regularly scheduled for mechanical cleaning
   is the
   A. large wrecker   B. Scout car
   C. Bombardier   D. Cushman Haulster

10. A hoist-fitted chassis is used MOST frequently to   10.__
    A. transport salt from one location to another
    B. collect refuse by gravity feeding into the truck's
       body
    C. flush streets and fight fires
    D. transport refuse containers to and from disposal
       locations

11. The capacity of the largest refuse collection truck now   11.__
    in use in the department is approximately _____ cubic yards.
    A. 20   B. 30   C. 40   D. 50

12. The one of the following pieces of manual equipment which   12.__
    would be IMPROPER to use in street cleaning is a
    A. pan scraper   B. short length of hose
    C. stillson wrench   D. scoop shovel

13. According to the department, an example of *avoidable dirt*   13.___
    is
    A. scrapings of concrete road paving as a result of
       roadwear
    B. a cigarette pack dropped from a moving vehicle
    C. a bolt that dropped from the muffler assembly of a
       car
    D. tire scrapings from the tread of a tire

14. The number of times a week that the highways, parkways,   14.___
    and expressways should be mechanically swept (other than
    for special attention conditions) is _____ a week.
    A. once   B. twice
    C. three times   D. four times

15. The one of the following seasons during which the vacuum   15.___
    leaf loader would MOST likely be used is
    A. summer   B. fall   C. winter   D. spring

16. Water is NOT ordinarily used in a cleaning operation to   16.___
    A. lay down dust in conjunction with machine sweeping
    B. wash streets in a regular machine flushing action
    C. clear streets of dirt during a drought
    D. flush the street in conjunction with a hydrant
       flushing action

17. The department collects garbage from all of the following   17.___
    categories of buildings and occupants EXCEPT
    A. residential occupants of residential buildings
    B. all occupants of public buildings
    C. commercial occupants of residential buildings
    D. tax-exempt buildings used for religious purposes

18. According to the department, tin cans are classified as   18.___
    waste material in the category of
    A. garbage   B. rubbish   C. junk   D. trash

19. The one of the following statements concerning trade   19.___
    waste that is CORRECT is:
    A. Building materials such as sheet rock and plywood
       are not considered to be trade waste
    B. A *trade waste premises* must pay the department an
       extra fee for regular collection service
    C. If the loaders of a collection truck are not sure
       whether the debris they are about to load is trade
       waste, they should collect it without incident
    D. It is a violation of the department's rules to
       remove trade waste from any premises

20. The one of the following arteries that is a SECONDARY   20.___
    street is one that is
    A. considered an old law tenement house street
    B. an expressway
    C. a feeder approach to a bridge
    D. a one-lane street with a police station on it

21. Suppose that a small amount of spillage occurs as a collection crew empties a garbage can into the collection truck.
The one of the following courses of action that the crew SHOULD take is to
    A. pick it up, using the brooms and shovel that are part of the truck's equipment
    B. wait for a sanitation man on foot duty to sweep it up
    C. push it neatly to the curb, to be collected by the next collection truck
    D. pick up anything lightweight with your hands, and leave the rest in its place

21.__

22. Preventive maintenance of motor equipment is usually accomplished in four stages, each designated by a different letter.
A 45-day inspection and lubrication is classified as Class
    A. A   B. B   C. C   D. D

22.__

23. In regard to compaction of refuse, it is CORRECT to state that compaction
    A. *increases* both the volume and the density of refuse
    B. *reduces* the volume of the refuse and increases the density
    C. *reduces* both the volume and density of refuse
    D. *increases* the volume of refuse and decreases the density

23.__

24. The classification of vehicle body used for transporting the contents of septic tanks is Class
    A. 1   B. 3   C. 5   D. 6

24.__

25. A function NOT normally that of the auxiliary field force is
    A. administering the functions of the lot cleaning force
    B. maintaining storage at encumbrance yards
    C. removing large dead animals
    D. sanding streets

25.__

KEY (CORRECT ANSWERS)

1. C	6. A	11. B	16. C	21. A
2. B	7. A	12. C	17. C	22. B
3. D	8. A	13. B	18. B	23. B
4. D	9. D	14. A	19. D	24. C
5. C	10. D	15. B	20. A	25. D

TEST 2

1. The alternate-side-of-the-street parking arrangement calls   1.___
   for the curbs to be free of parked cars from _____ times
   a week.
   A. 1 to 3   B. 3 to 5   C. 5 to 7   D. 2 to 6

2. A piece of department equipment which rolls on rubber   2.___
   tires instead of caterpillar treads is the
   A. athey wagon   B. crawler tractor
   C. front end loader   D. bombardier

3. Of the following statements concerning the department's   3.___
   collection trucks, the one which is TRUE is that
   A. compactor trucks constitute the greatest portion of
      the fleet
   B. front loading collection trucks generally have smaller
      capacities than rear loading trucks
   C. the smallest size collection truck has a capacity of
      15 cubic yards
   D. compactor trucks should not be used for the collec-
      tion of ashes

4. The department's do-it-yourself depots are open   4.___
   A. only on weekdays
   B. only Monday through Saturday
   C. seven days a week except for legal holidays
   D. seven days a week including holidays

5. The spacing of litter baskets is related to the density   5.___
   of pedestrian traffic.
   The priority description for litter baskets placed one
   for every 100 feet minimum is _____ pedestrian traffic.
   A. heavy   B. medium   C. light   D. all

6. Suppose you are new in a command and you have to assign   6.___
   street cleaning equipment on a particular day.
   For you to take into account the fact that a street may
   or may not have a curb is a
   A. *good* idea, because uncurbed streets must be cleaned
      by the owner of the property abutting that street
   B. *poor* idea, because there are more important factors
      to consider
   C. *good* idea, because consideration of curbing affects
      the type of equipment being used
   D. *poor* idea, because your men will work just as fast
      regardless of the presence of a curb

7. Filled collection trucks entering a marine transfer sta- 7.__
   tion are weighed before dumping.
   A record is made of each load dumped PRIMARILY to
   A. compare truck load statistics with those of other
      stations
   B. compare the weight of each load with the previous
      load
   C. determine the total tonnage of waste put onto the
      scows
   D. determine whether the trucks are fully loaded

8. An incinerator plant is *usually* under the DIRECT super- 8.__
   vision of a
   A. stationary engineer
   B. senior stationary engineer
   C. section foreman
   D. district superintendent

9. At an incinerator plant, the one of the following actions 9.__
   that occurs LAST is that the driver of a filled collec-
   tion truck
   A. drives the truck onto the tipping floor
   B. drives the truck onto the scale
   C. dumps the truck's load into the storage pit
   D. hands in the truck's load ticket

10. At the mechanical feed furnaces, the hot residue is   10.__
    quenched by
    A. being sprinkled with water
    B. being partially submerged in water
    C. a combination of forced air drying and sprinkling
       with water
    D. being completely submerged in water

11. The compartments of garbage scows are *sounded* in order to 11.__
    determine whether
    A. there are defects in the wall of the scow
    B. water is present in the compartments
    C. the scow is fully loaded
    D. any parts of the scow are missing

12. The average marine transfer station loads two barges a   12.__
    day.
    The number of truckloads that this is EQUAL to is
    approximately
    A. 125   B. 175   C. 250   D. 325

13. The marine transfer stations that do not have exhaust fans 13.__
    are equipped to sprinkle fine sprays of water over the
    waste in scows in order to _____ the scow.
    A. put out any fires on   B. liquify any dirt on
    C. remove odors from   D. lay the dust on

14. The aft of a barge is the   14._____
    A. rear end   B. front end
    C. right side   D. left side

15. The machine used to move the barges into position to be   15._____
unloaded is the
    A. barge digger   B. athey wagon
    C. gypsy engine   D. tractor

16. A large supermarket's refrigeration machinery breaks down 16._____
on a hot weekend which results in the spoilage of hundreds of pounds of food. The supermarket's owner con-
tacts a private cartman and then proceeds to have the
putrified food piled on the sidewalk outside the store.
According to the health code, this action by the owner is
    A. *illegal* under any conditions
    B. *legal only* if the goods are removed within a maximum
       of three hours by the cartman
    C. *legal only* if the goods are removed within a maximum
       of twelve hours by the cartman
    D. *legal only* if the goods are removed within a maximum
       of twenty-four hours by the cartman

17. A private land owner acquires some quantities of clean   17._____
concrete, ashes, rock, and sand which he wishes to use
as a fill on his land.
If he has the necessary permits, the materials which he
is allowed to incorporate into his fill, according to the
health code, are
    A. the concrete and sand *only*
    B. the sand and rock *only*
    C. the sand, rock, and ashes *only*
    D. all of the materials he acquired

18. Of the following acts, the one which is PERMITTED by the 18._____
health code is
    A. walking a dog on a six-foot leash on a public side-
       walk
    B. handing out commercial handbills on a street corner
       to passersby
    C. beating a rug in a courtyard of an apartment house
    D. dumping noxious liquids into a public sewer

19. A tenant of a large apartment house has removed some old 19._____
furniture to be picked up by the department's bulk collection service. A junkman arrives and the tenant asks
him if he wants to take the discarded furniture instead.
According to the administrative code, if the junkman
complies with the tenant's request, _____ violated the
administrative code.
    A. *both* the tenant and the junkman have
    B. *only* the tenant has
    C. *only* the junkman has
    D. *neither* party has

20. Private carters need licenses and permits to transport   20.
    various classes of waste.
    The one of the following classes that requires a permit
    from the department of health is Class
        A. 1   B. 2   C. 3   D. 4

21. When a tenant is evicted from a building, any encumbrance   21.
    resulting may be stored in facilities maintained by the
    department.
    If these encumbrances are held in storage for 30 days or
    more, the goods are
        A. automatically returned to the owner
        B. burned and used for landfill
        C. inspected to determine suitability for donation to
           charity
        D. subject to sale by auction

22. Of the following, the FIRST step you should take in the   22.
    first aid treatment for a second-degree chemical skin
    burn is to
        A. cover it with bandages
        B. break the blisters
        C. apply antiseptic ointment
        D. apply large amounts of cold water

23. To *safely* lift a heavy object from the ground, you should   23.
    keep your arms and elbows
        A. *away* from the body with your back bent
        B. *away* from the body with your back straight
        C. *close* to the body with your back bent
        D. *close* to the body with your back straight

24. A symptom of heat exhaustion is   24.
        A. heavy perspiration   B. dry skin
        C. numbness   D. foaming at the mouth

25. Of the following firefighting agents used in portable   25.
    fire extinguishers, the one which is MOST likely to
    spread a flammable liquid fire is
        A. foam   B. a solid stream of water
        C. carbon dioxide   D. dry chemical

KEY (CORRECT ANSWERS)

1. A	6. C	11. B	16. A	21. D
2. C	7. C	12. C	17. D	22. D
3. A	8. B	13. D	18. A	23. D
4. D	9. C	14. A	19. D	24. A
5. A	10. D	15. C	20. D	25. B

EXAMINATION SECTION
TEST 1

DIRECTIONS: Each question or incomplete statement is followed by several suggested answers or completions. Select the one that BEST answers the question or completes the statement. *PRINT THE LETTER OF THE CORRECT ANSWER IN THE SPACE AT THE RIGHT.*

1. You are following up on the inspections which have been made by one of your inspectors whose work is usually satisfactory. You visit an establishment recently inspected by him and note several violations of the Code which the inspector had failed to report. You discuss the matter with the inspector who becomes highly indignant and insists that the establishment complied with the provisions of the Code at the time of his inspection. Under the circumstances, it would be MOST advisable for you to state that   1._____

    A. a report of the incident, submitted to the borough chief, will be included in the inspector's personnel file
    B. at the time of your visit the premises did not comply with some of the provisions of the Code
    C. future failure to report violations of the Code will be regarded as presumptive evidence of collusion
    D. you will recommend a transfer or termination of the employment of the inspector if the situation occurs again

2. You have been assigned to spotcheck the daily report of an inspector. The inspector has indicated that he inspected a certain establishment at 3 P.M. The owner of the establishment insists that the inspector inspected his premises at 11 A.M.
Of the following courses of action, you should FIRST   2._____

    A. interview the owners of the establishment visited by the inspector before and after the establishment in question
    B. secure the inspector's daily report for the previous day and check every stop on that report
    C. telephone the inspector to determine the actual time of his visit
    D. write a formal memorandum to the borough chief regarding the incident

3. You are investigating the complaint made by the owner of an establishment who alleged that an inspector spoke to him in a loud and disrespectful manner while inspecting his premises. You interview the complainant and ask him if he has any witnesses to support his complaint. He tells you that he does not. You note that the inspector found several violations of the Code in the course of his inspection of the premises.
Under these circumstances, you should   3._____

    A. assure the owner that in the interest of good public relations the inspector involved will not be assigned to inspect the owner's premises in the future
    B. discuss the matter with the inspector before submitting your report
    C. inform the owner that complaints which cannot be substantiated cannot receive further consideration
    D. mark the complaint *not substantiated* and refrain from discussing it with the inspector

4. You are assigned to work with another inspector on a complex inspectional problem   4.__
   which has received considerable newspaper publicity. After the field work is completed,
   you agree to prepare a report incorporating both findings. You prepare the report and
   submit it directly to your superior without showing it to your fellow inspector. At a staff
   conference, your superior praises your report and the work performed by you; he mini-
   mizes the performance of your fellow inspector. You remain silent. Later you learn that
   your fellow inspector has been aggrieved by your conduct.
   Of the following courses of action, it is MOST advisable that you

   A. ask the inspector whether he wishes you to try to get more credit for him
   B. discuss the matter with your fellow inspector and later with your superior to point
      out that the inspection was a joint effort and that your colleague should share in the
      credit
   C. ignore the matter and allow time to take care of the incident
   D. write a memorandum to your superior detailing precisely the work performed by
      the other inspector in connection with the assignment

5. Assume that you are a licensed pharmacist and would like to secure a part-time job as a   5.__
   pharmacist to supplement your income. In the course of your work as an inspector, you
   investigate an anonymous complaint against a drug store. Your investigation discloses
   nothing to indicate that the drug store owner has violated any provision of the Code. The
   owner, learning that you are a licensed pharmacist, asks you to work for him on a part-
   time basis. Under the circumstances, you SHOULD

   A. *accept* provided that the owner has not asked you for special consideration
   B. *accept* provided that you will receive the union scale of wages
   C. *refuse* the offer since a conflict of interest situation may be involved
   D. *refuse* the offer until you have a chance to discuss it with other inspectors who are
      licensed pharmacists

6. Your supervisor frequently bypasses you and assigns work directly to your subordinates.   6.__
   You had called this matter to his attention previously. At that time, he assured you that
   you would not be bypassed again. However, he has continued to bypass you.
   Under these circumstances, you SHOULD

   A. attempt to determine the reasons for your supervisor's action before proceeding
      further
   B. begin keeping a record of the instances when you are bypassed, and forward a
      memorandum to your supervisor's superior setting forth such instances
   C. ignore the situation until such time as your supervisor brings the matter up for dis-
      cussion
   D. instruct your staff that they are to accept assignments only from you

7. In checking the daily reports of one of your inspectors, you notice that he is consistently   7.__
   late in beginning his working day. You discuss the matter with him and point out that disciplinary action may be taken unless he starts work promptly. He denies that he is tardy
   in beginning his work day. However, based on your field follow-up visits, the evidence
   indicates that the inspector continues to be late in starting work. Again, you discuss the
   matter with him and he again denies your contention that he is late in starting work.
   You should

A. again point out the need for starting work promptly and continue checking the inspector's starting time
B. discuss the matter with other inspectors in the work group to get their advice
C. ignore the matter as long as the inspector makes about as many inspections as others in the group
D. report the inspector to your supervisor for appropriate disciplinary action

8. One of the inspectors in your group makes about one-fourth more inspections than any other inspector. However, his inspections do not meet satisfactory standards of quality. After you have given him training in the field, his work improves to a point where it is satisfactory. However, he still makes about one-fourth more inspections than any of the other inspectors.
You should

   A. ask that the inspector be transferred to a unit where the quantity and quality of work produced by him will be closer to the group standard
   B. ask the proprietors of establishments visited by this inspector whether the inspections were too cursory
   C. devote less time to this inspector so that you may devote more time to those inspectors who may need additional training
   D. instruct the inspector to reduce the number of his inspections to the group standard and spend more time in each establishment

9. Assume that your superior has given you an additional job to do which will require extra effort on the part of your inspectors who are now carrying a full work load. You feel that the job cannot be completed in the allotted time. You present your point of view but your superior insists that you handle the assignment without any increase in staff.
Of the following courses of action, it would be MOST advisable for you to

   A. attempt to complete the assignment within the allotted time by rescheduling and re-assigning other work
   B. commit yourself to no specific course of action while attempting to secure evidence to support your position that you should not be given the assignment
   C. insist that your superior give you some assurance that this assignment does not set a precedent for assignments of a similar nature and agree to do the job
   D. take the matter up with higher authority, preferably by memorandum, but apprise your superior of your action

10. You are conducting a conference with the inspectors assigned to you. During the conference, you make a statement regarding field inspections which you are reasonably certain is correct. One of the inspectors tells you in an offensive manner that your statement is incorrect. Some of the inspectors agree with him; others remain silent. Under these circumstances, you SHOULD

   A. ask the inspectors who have not made any comments for their opinions and be guided by their remarks
   B. ignore the offensive manner of the speaker and state that since you are certain that you are correct, the group will be guided by your statement
   C. state that while the manner of the speaker is offensive he is nevertheless probably correct
   D. state that you will ascertain whether your statement is correct and will advise them of it in the near future

11. Assume that you are in the habit of writing to your supervisor on subjects related to your duties. Your supervisor tells you that you are writing too many memorandums to him. Of the following courses of action, it is MOST preferable for you to

    A. instruct your inspectors not to put in writing communications regarding the work of the unit
    B. refrain from communicating in writing with your supervisor
    C. take no notice of your supervisor's statement since the smooth functioning of an organization depends upon written communication
    D. write to your supervisor only when you feel that it is necessary

11._

12. You are accompanying one of your recently appointed inspectors on a field inspection. His inspections take an unusually long time to complete since he is extremely meticulous.
In these circumstances, you should FIRST

    A. assure the inspector of your confidence in his ability to perform his job properly after sufficient training before criticizing his work performance
    B. seek the transfer of the inspector to a position in the department which does not require contact with the public
    C. tell the inspector that if he does not bring his work up to standard immediately, you will report him to your supervisor
    D. urge the inspector to seek employment in a field not related to his present work

12._

13. A rumor has started among the members of your staff to the effect that you will soon be leaving government service to take a position in private industry. You know that the rumor is untrue.
You SHOULD

    A. ask your staff not to discuss matters among themselves which relate to your own affairs
    B. inform your staff that you do not intend to take a position in private industry
    C. say nothing about the matter to your staff
    D. tell your staff that you refuse to confirm or deny rumors concerning your employment prospects

13._

14. You request an inspector to do something in a certain manner. The inspector asks you the reason for performing the operation in the manner suggested by you.
You SHOULD

    A. change the subject of your discussion
    B. explain to the inspector that it is his job to carry out instructions - not to evaluate them
    C. give the inspector the reason for your request
    D. tell the inspector that if he thinks about the matter he will be able to determine the reason himself

14._

15. You are conducting a conference with your staff. One of your inspectors seems completely disinterested in the discussion.
To get this inspector to participate, you SHOULD

    A. ask the inspector direct questions related to the subject being discussed
    B. determine if there is any subject this inspector would like the group to discuss

15._

C. ignore the situation until such time as the inspector shows interest
D. tell the inspector in a polite way to pay strict attention

16. You are conducting a conference with your staff and are having a great deal of difficulty with one of the inspectors who wants to do all of the talking. You have previously spoken privately to this inspector regarding his habit of *hogging the discussion*—to no avail. Under the circumstances, you SHOULD

    16.____

    A. ask the inspector to act as an auditor only during conferences
    B. elicit discussion by direct questioning of other members of the staff
    C. refrain from looking at the inspector when you ask a question; this will make it impossible for him to *get the floor*
    D. tell the inspector to remain silent or to leave the group

17. You telephone one of your inspectors, assigning him to the central office for a period of two days to perform clerical duties. The inspector complains loudly, tells you that he dislikes clerical work and that he is being treated unfairly since there are inspectors in other boroughs who are assigned less frequently to clerical duties. You explain the situation as best you can but the inspector continues to object.
Under these circumstances, you SHOULD

    17.____

    A. ask the inspector to disregard the assignment pending your inquiry into practices followed in other boroughs in assigning personnel to clerical duties
    B. promise the inspector that in the future you will do your best to give clerical assignments to people who do not voice objections to such assignments
    C. tell the inspector to report for duty in accordance with your instructions
    D. tell the inspector to take the matter up with your superior

18. In developing an on-the-job training program for inspectors, the FIRST thing which should be determined is

    18.____

    A. areas in which training is needed
    B. how many inspectors are interested in training
    C. how much will the training program cost
    D. what training aids and facilities are available

19. Assume that a recently appointed and inexperienced inspector is given a difficult assignment. He is not given any specific instructions as to how the assignment should be carried out.
Such action is

    19.____

    A. *good;* a new employee needs to be encouraged to exercise his own initiative
    B. *good;* a new employee will remember longer if he learns by himself
    C. *poor;* newly appointed employees usually need guidance
    D. *poor;* the cost of training varies from employee to employee

20. A number of important changes have taken place in several sections of the Code. You are to inform a group of inspectors of these changes and how they are to be implemented. While speaking to the group concerning the changes, one of the inspectors whom you know to be a quick learner complains that you are proceeding too slowly; another inspector whom you know to be the slowest learner in the group tells you that your teaching pace
is just right. You SHOULD

    20.____

A. bring the session to a halt and instruct group members on an individual basis
B. proceed at a faster rate
C. proceed at a faster rate but allow more time for *breaks*
D. proceed at the same rate

21. As part of a new inspector's training, you observe him as he conducts an inspection. The inspector completes the *score-card* on which he lists certain violations of the Code. You look at the *score-card* and note that although the inspector spoke to the establishment owner about a certain violation, the inspector failed to list the violation on the *score-card*. Of the following, the MOST desirable way of pointing out this omission is to

    21.__

A. ask the inspector to look at the *score-card* to see if anything is missing
B. criticize the inspector in a forthright manner and impress upon him the importance of the probationary period
C. show the *score-card* to the owner and ask the owner to indicate the violation which was noted but not recorded
D. tell the inspector in the presence of the owner to list the violation and make a separate note of the omission for service rating purposes

22. Assume that you are in the field training a recently appointed inspector in inspectional techniques.
The inspections demonstrated by you SHOULD be of the kind

    22.__

A. consistent with the high standards of experienced inspectors
B. performed by the average beginning inspector so as not to unduly discourage the trainee
C. performed by the sanitarian who barely meets the minimum acceptable standard
D. which varies sharply from one inspection to the next so that the new inspector will be able to familiarize himself with various ways in which inspections may be conducted

23. The one of the following which LEAST describes the function of planning at the senior inspector level of supervision is deciding

    23.__

A. *how* something should be done
B. *what* must be done
C. *who* should do it
D. *why* something should be done

24. For effective management, delegation of responsibility MUST be accompanied by *appropriate*

    24.__

A. authority
B. commendation
C. compensation
D. privilege

25. The one of the following which is LEAST a *staff* function in an organization is

    25.__

A. advising   B. directing   C. observing   D. planning

26. Assume that an employee is responsible to two supervisors of equal rank for the proper performance of his duties. The principle of good management which is NOT being complied with is

    26.__

A. delegation of authority
B. fixed responsibility
C. homogeneous assignment
D. unity of command

27. Where low morale is responsible for low work output, the FIRST step which should be taken is to

    27.____

    A. determine the reason for the poor state of morale by interviewing supervisors and employees who are directly affected
    B. have the head of the organization deliver an inspirational talk to those responsible for the low work output, stressing the mission of the organization and the importance of the work involved
    C. lower standards of production to equal work output and then gradually increase these standards to the desired level
    D. withdraw privileges with regard to the granting of leave, coffee breaks, and choice of lunch hours until work output rises to a satisfactory level

28. The one of the following which is NOT usually a need which gives rise to a work simplification program in government is the need to

    28.____

    A. make the job as pleasant as possible for employees
    B. make things more convenient for members of the public
    C. produce a greater quantity and higher quality of work
    D. provide additional employment in times of recession

29. The MOST practical control the inspector has over the contractor when the inspector is not satisfied with the quality of the work is to

    29.____

    A. discuss withholding payment on that part of the work that is unsatisfactory
    B. threaten to have the contractor thrown off the job
    C. request that the contractor fire the men responsible for the unsatisfactory work
    D. call the owner of the company and explain the situation to him

30. In the absence of a formal training program for inspectors, the BEST of the following ways to train a new man who is to do inspection work is to

    30.____

    A. give him the literature on the subject so that he can learn what he has to know
    B. have him accompany an inspector as the inspector does his work so that he can learn by observing
    C. assign him the job and let him learn on his own
    D. tell him to go to a school at night that specializes in this field so that he will gain the necessary background

KEY (CORRECT ANSWERS)

1.	B		16.	B
2.	A		17.	C
3.	B		18.	A
4.	B		19.	C
5.	C		20.	D
6.	A		21.	A
7.	D		22.	A
8.	C		23.	D
9.	A		24.	A
10.	D		25.	B
11.	D		26.	D
12.	A		27.	A
13.	B		28.	D
14.	C		29.	A
15.	A		30.	B

TEST 2

DIRECTIONS: Each question or incomplete statement is followed by several suggested answers or completions. Select the one that BEST answers the question or completes the statement. *PRINT THE LETTER OF THE CORRECT ANSWER IN THE SPACE AT THE RIGHT.*

1. Assume that you are a supervisor newly assigned to a squad of inspectors. In order to establish a favorable working atmosphere, it is BEST to   1._____

   A. discipline ineffective members of your squad at regular intervals
   B. speak extensively on job-related subjects
   C. give advice on personal matters
   D. recognize and accept ideas submitted by members of your squad

2. Assume that you are a supervisor who has in his squad an ambitious inspector studying for promotion. This man takes every opportunity to ask you questions about your job. Under the circumstances, it is BEST for you to   2._____

   A. remind him firmly that he already has a full-time job and that if he wishes to study for promotion he should do it off-duty by himself
   B. plan your time so that you can assist in his promotional aspirations
   C. tell him that you would like to help but that you do not wish to give him an advantage over others
   D. resist instructing him because if he is promoted you will lose a valuable man, thereby weakening your squad

3. A signed written complaint has been mailed directly to you alleging that one of your inspectors has been overly aggressive in that he pushed the complainant. The inspector is a good worker, and this is the first complaint ever recorded against him. Under the circumstances, it is BEST to   3._____

   A. notify informally the accused inspector of the nature of the complaint, and suggest that he guard his behavior in the future
   B. ignore the complaint as being too vague to warrant action
   C. have the complainant carefully investigated to see whether he has made similar complaints in the past
   D. have the complaint investigated by someone disinterested in the outcome of the matter

4. Assume that you are a supervisor in charge of an inspector who has a good work record but who, for the first time, exhibits symptoms of drunkenness. When confronted, he denies that he ever drinks and says that his apparently intoxicated behavior is really the result of his doctor's medication for the flu. Under the circumstances, it is BEST to   4._____

   A. ignore the situation for the present but later report the matter to your superiors
   B. tell the man that you know he's untruthful but that, because of his previous good record, you are willing to overlook his condition this time
   C. accept the man's explanation, send him home for the day on sick leave, but watch for future symptoms of possible drunken behavior
   D. reprimand the man, send out for coffee to sober him up, and warn him the next time he exhibits drunken symptoms he will face severe disciplinary action

5. Assume that you are in charge of a squad of inspectors. One inspector has been per-   5.__
forming ineffectively, although working hard. All attempts to improve his performance
have failed. He is nearing the end of his probationary period.
In the circumstances, it is BEST to

    A. reschedule assignments so that the rest of the squad takes over a greater share of
the work load
    B. recommend separation on the ground that improvement cannot be achieved
    C. assign only the simplest cases to the man
    D. leave the man alone, since he seems to be doing the best he can

6. As a supervisor, you have been instructed by your superiors to install a radically revised   6.__
system of procedure for your squad. You are concerned that your subordinates may
resist the change.
The BEST way for you to secure the willing cooperation of your squad in effecting the
change is to

    A. secure the participation of all your subordinates in planning for the change, empha-
sizing the absence of any threat to their security
    B. *sell* your subordinates on the new procedure by emphasizing that the procedure
has the full backing of your superiors
    C. warn your subordinates not to sabotage the change, emphasizing that willful inter-
ference with the change will be followed by severe corrective disciplinary action
    D. appeal to your subordinates' loyalty to the agency and to yourself, emphasizing
that *one hand washes the other*

7. Supervising inspectors are involved in the decision-making process.   7._
Effective decision-making means MOST NEARLY

    A. compromising, since all decisions involve compromise
    B. selecting the course of action with the least unexpected consequences
    C. holding off on any action until circumstances dictate one particular approach
    D. securing employee participation in the planning and policy process

8. Assume that you are a supervisor in charge of an inspector who may be abusing sick   8._
leave.
Under the circumstances, the FIRST thing you should do is to

    A. interview the inspector to find out what is wrong
    B. maintain a calendar of sick leave used by the inspector to see whether a pattern
develops indicating abuse
    C. warn the inspector against any further malingering
    D. institute corrective disciplinary action the very next time the inspector reports sick

9. Supervision is a social relationship. It is both the art of being a leader and a subordinate.   9.
This statement implies that

    A. the supervisory relationship involves an expectation of obedience on the part of the
supervisor and a willingness to obey on the part of the subordinate
    B. the really successful supervisor always knows that his subordinates understand
him, and doesn't have to clarify and explain his orders
    C. in the supervisory relationship, supervisor and subordinate should strive to be as
friendly with each other as possible

D. the really wise subordinate knows his job and sees to it that his supervisor knows that he knows his job

10. As a supervising inspector, you have a man in your squad who avoids difficult tasks on the ground that he cannot do the more difficult work. You have informally condoned this practice because he is effective and busy on lesser tasks, overall squad production is satisfactory, and no one has complained. Nevertheless, you decide to review the situation.
Solely on the basis of the information presented, the LEAST effective response to this situation is to

10.____

    A. denounce the man before the group and ask for their advice on handling the matter
    B. insist on a basic work capability for all members of the squad
    C. continue the present practice informally, so long as production and morale are unaffected
    D. remind the man that professional recognition awaits those who work hard on a variety of tasks

11. Assume that you are a new supervisor in charge of a squad of inspectors. Your superior informs you that the squad has long been declining in effectiveness. Your job is to increase production without changing personnel.
Of the following, the MOST important information for you to have in order to effect change is

11.____

    A. the reason for the squad's past production successes
    B. an accurate account of your squad's present state of mind
    C. a knowledge of the interplay of psychic needs and neighborhood surroundings in producing the squad's laxity
    D. a case history on every individual so that you can estimate the personal impact of prospective changes

12. Assume that you have become the supervisor of a high morale squad of inspectors, all of whom are experienced and productive.
The BEST supervisory approach for you to take to insure the continuance of an efficient squad is to

12.____

    A. *leave them alone,* since it doesn't pay to tinker with a well-running mechanism
    B. develop a close personal relationship with the most experienced member of your squad and use this relationship to govern the rest of the squad
    C. take charge immediately, and let them know who's in charge since everything usually runs well when persons are alert
    D. work problems out together, on the theory that things usually run well when the supervisor successfully seeks to build power with, rather than hold authority over, his work group

13. One of the things a supervising inspector should AVOID doing is

13.____

    A. answering unimportant questions asked by the public
    B. talking to people he does not know
    C. blaming his supervisors for all the unpleasant orders the supervising inspector must issue
    D. showing an interest in public problems

14. An angry building owner complains loudly to you, the supervisor, about the actions of the   14._
    inspectors assigned to you.
    You should

    A. try to find excuses for your men's actions
    B. speak to him in the same tone of voice he is using
    C. insist that the actions of your men are correct
    D. try to answer his complaint quietly

15. In dealing with the general public, an inspector should remember that   15._

    A. every person is an individual who may think for himself
    B. all people tend to think alike
    C. most people think alike
    D. it is best to change the public's way of thinking to what the department requires

16. An inspector is performing his job in the BEST manner when he   16._

    A. continually checks with his supervisor to make sure each inspection is being done
       properly
    B. knows enough to overlook minor violations that have a negligible effect on overall
    C. varies the rules when he feels they do not meet the conditions of the job
    D. is careful and observant in his inspections

17. An IMPORTANT characteristic of a good supervisor is his ability to   17._

    A. be a stern disciplinarian
    B. put off the settling of grievances
    C. solve problems
    D. find fault in individuals

18. At the time you hand out a job assignment, an inspector feels that he cannot complete   18._
    the job within the time limit you have given him.
    You would expect the inspector FIRST to

    A. make as many inspections as possible and then report to you
    B. compare his workload to that of the other inspectors
    C. complete the work by putting in overtime before notifying you of the problem
    D. request assistance in doing the work

19. A new supervising inspector will BEST obtain the respect of the men assigned to him if   19._
    he

    A. makes decisions rapidly and sticks to them regardless of whether they are right or
       wrong
    B. makes decisions rapidly and then changes them just as rapidly if the decisions are
       wrong
    C. does not make decisions unless he is absolutely sure that they are right
    D. makes his decisions after considering carefully all available information

20. A newly-appointed inspector is operating at a level of performance below that of the   20.
    other employees.
    In this situation, a supervisor should FIRST

A. lower the acceptable standard for the new inspector
B. find out why the new inspector cannot do as well as the others
C. advise the new inspector he will be dropped from the payroll at the end of the probationary period
D. assign another new inspector to assist the first inspector

21. Assume that you have to instruct a new inspector on a specific departmental operation. The new man seems unsure of what you have said.
Of the following, the BEST way for you to determine whether the man has understood you is to

21.____

A. have the man explain the operation to you in his own words
B. repeat your explanation to him slowly
C. repeat your explanation to him, using simpler wording
D. emphasize the important parts of the operation to him

22. A supervising inspector realizes that he has taken an instantaneous dislike to a new inspector assigned to him. The BEST course of action for this supervisor to take in this case is to

22.____

A. be especially observant of the new inspector's actions
B. request that the new inspector be reassigned
C. make a special effort to be fair to the new inspector
D. ask to be transferred himself

23. A supervisor gives detailed instructions to his inspectors as to how a certain type of job is to be done.
One ADVANTAGE of this practice is that this will

23.____

A. result in a more flexible operation
B. standardize operations
C. encourage new men to learn
D. encourage initiative in the men

24. Of the following, the one that would MOST likely be the result of poor planning is:

24.____

A. Omissions are discovered after the work is completed
B. During the course of normal inspection, a meter is found to be unaccessible
C. An inspector completes his assignments for that day ahead of schedule
D. A problem arises during an inspection, and prevents an inspector from completing his day's assignments

25. Of the following, the BEST way for a supervisor to maintain good morale among his inspectors is for the supervisor to

25.____

A. avoid correcting an inspector when he makes mistakes
B. continually praise an inspector's work even when it is of average quality
C. show that he is willing to assist in solving the inspector's problems
D. accept the inspector's excuses for failure even though the excuses are not valid

KEY (CORRECT ANSWERS)

1.	D	11.	B
2.	B	12.	D
3.	D	13.	C
4.	C	14.	D
5.	B	15.	A
6.	A	16.	D
7.	B	17.	C
8.	A	18.	D
9.	A	19.	D
10.	A	20.	B

21.	A
22.	C
23.	B
24.	A
25.	C

———

EXAMINATION SECTION
TEST 1

DIRECTIONS: Each question or incomplete statement is followed by several suggested answers or completions. Select the one that BEST answers the question or completes the statement. *PRINT THE LETTER OF THE CORRECT ANSWER IN THE SPACE AT THE RIGHT.*

Questions 1-4.

DIRECTIONS: Questions 1 through 4 are to be answered on the basis of the information provided in the paragraph below.

Rodent control must be planned carefully in order to insure its success. This means that more knowledge is needed about the habits and favorite breeding places of Domestic Rats, than any other kind. A favorite breeding place for Domestic Rats is known to be in old or badly constructed buildings. Rats find these buildings very comfortable for making nests. However, the only way to gain this kind of detailed knowledge about rats is through careful study.

1. According to the above paragraph, rats find comfortable nesting places   1._____

   A. in old buildings   B. in pipes
   C. on roofs   D. in sewers

2. The paragraph states that the BEST way to learn all about the favorite nesting places of rats is by   2._____

   A. asking people   B. careful study
   C. using traps   D. watching ratholes

3. According to the paragraph, in order to insure the success of rodent control, it is necessary to   3._____

   A. design better bait   B. give out more information
   C. plan carefully   D. use pesticides

4. The paragraph states that the MOST important rats to study are _____ rats.   4._____

   A. African   B. Asian   C. Domestic   D. European

Questions 5-8.

DIRECTIONS: Questions 5 through 8 are to be answered on the basis of the following paragraph.

A few people who live in old tenements have the bad habit of throwing garbage out of their windows, especially if there is an empty lot near their building. Sometimes the garbage is food, sometimes the garbage is half-empty soda cans. Sometimes the garbage is a little bit of both mixed together. These people just don't care about keeping the lot clean.

5. The paragraph states that throwing garbage out of windows is a

    A. bad habit
    B. dangerous thing to do
    C. good thing to do
    D. good way to feed rats

6. According to the paragraph, an empty lot next to an old tenement is sometimes used as a place to

    A. hold local gang meetings
    B. play ball
    C. throw garbage
    D. walk dogs

7. According to the paragraph, which of the following throw garbage out of their windows?

    A. Nobody
    B. Everybody
    C. Most people
    D. Some people

8. According to the paragraph, the kinds of garbage thrown out of windows are

    A. candy and cigarette butts
    B. food and half-empty soda cans
    C. fruit and vegetables
    D. rice and bread

Questions 9-12.

DIRECTIONS: Questions 9 through 12 are to be answered on the basis of the following paragraph.

   The game that is recognised all over the world as an all-American game is the game of baseball. As a matter of fact, baseball heroes like Joe DiMaggio, Willie Mays, and Babe Ruth, were as famous in their day as movie stars Robert Redford, Paul Newman, and Clint East-wood are now. All these men have had the experience of being mobbed by fans whenever they put in an appearance anywhere in the world. Such unusual popularity makes it possible for stars like these to earn at least as much money off the job as on the job. It didn't take man-ufacturers and advertising men long to discover that their sales of shaving lotion, for instance, increased when they got famous stars to advertise their product for them on radio and tele-vision.

9. According to the paragraph, baseball is known everywhere as a(n) _____ game.

    A. all-American
    B. fast
    C. unusual
    D. tough

10. According to the paragraph, being so well known means that it is possible for people like Willie Mays and Babe Ruth to

    A. ask for anything and get it
    B. make as much money off the job as on it
    C. travel anywhere free of charge
    D. watch any game free of charge

11. According to the paragraph, which of the following are known all over the world?

    A. Baseball heroes
    B. Advertising men
    C. Manufacturers
    D. Basketball heroes

12. According to the paragraph, it is possible to sell much more shaving lotion on television and radio if   12.____

   A. the commercials are in color instead of black and white
   B. you can get a prize with each bottle of shaving lotion
   C. the shaving lotion makes you smell nicer than usual
   D. the shaving lotion is advertised by famous stars

Questions 13-16.

DIRECTIONS: Questions 13 through 16 are to be answered on the basis of the following paragraph.

People are very suspicious of all strangers who knock at their door. For this reason, every pest control aide, whether man or woman, must carry an identification card at all times on the job. These cards are issued by the agency the aide works for. The aide's picture is on the card. The aide 's name is typed in, and the aide 's signature is written on the line below. The name, address, and telephone number of the agency issuing the card is also printed on it. Once the aide shows this ID card to prove his or her identity, the tenant's time should not be taken up with small talk. The tenant should be told briefly what pest control means. The aide should be polite and ready to answer any questions the tenant may have on the subject. Then, the aide should thank the tenant for listening and say goodbye.

13. According to the above paragraph, when she visits tenants, the one item a pest control aide must ALWAYS carry with her is a(n)   13.____

   A. badge   B. driver's license
   C. identification card   D. watch

14. According to the paragraph, a pest control aide is supposed to talk to each tenant he visits   14.____

   A. at length about the agency
   B. briefly about pest control
   C. at length about family matters
   D. briefly about social security

15. According to the paragraph, the item that does NOT appear on an ID card is the   15.____

   A. address of the agency
   B. name of the agency
   C. signature of the aide
   D. social security number of the aide

16. According to the paragraph, a pest control aide carries an identification card because he must   16.____

   A. prove to tenants who he is
   B. provide the tenants with the agency's address
   C. provide the tenant with the agency's telephone number
   D. save the tenant's time

Questions 17-20.

DIRECTIONS: Questions 17 through 20 are to be answered on the basis of the following paragraph.

Very early on a summer's morning, the nicest thing to look at is a beach, before the swimmers arrive. Usually all the litter has been picked up from the sand by the Park Department clean-up crew. Everything is quiet. All you can hear are the waves breaking, and the sea gulls calling to each other. The beach opens to the public at 10 A.M. Long before that time, however, long lines of eager men, women, and children have driven up to the entrance. They form long lines that wind around the beach waiting for the signal to move.

17. According to the paragraph, before 10 A.M., long lines are formed that are made up of   17____

    A. cars   B. clean-up crews
    C. men, women, and children   D. Park Department trucks

18. The season referred to in the above paragraph is   18____

    A. fall   B. summer   C. winter   D. spring

19. The place the paragraph is describing is a   19____

    A. beach   B. park
    C. golf course   D. tennis court

20. According to the paragraph, one of the things you notice early in the morning is that   20____

    A. radios are playing   B. swimmers are there
    C. the sand is dirty   D. the litter is gone

Questions 21-30.

DIRECTIONS: In Questions 21 through 30, select the answer which means MOST NEARLY the SAME as the capitalized word in the sentence.

21. He received a large REWARD.   21____
In this sentence, the word REWARD means

    A. capture   B. recompense
    C. key   D. praise

22. The aide was asked to TRANSMIT a message. In this sentence, the word TRANSMIT   22____
means

    A. change   B. send   C. take   D. type

23. The pest control aide REQUESTED the tenant to call the Health Department.   23____
In this sentence, the word REQUESTED means the pest control aide

    A. asked   B. helped   C. informed   D. warned

24. The driver had to RETURN the Health Department's truck. In this sentence, the word   24____
RETURN means

    A. borrow   B. fix   C. give back   D. load up

25. The aide discussed the PURPOSE of the visit. In this sentence, the word PURPOSE means   25.____

    A. date   B. hour   C. need   D. reason,

26. The tenant SUSPECTED the aide who knocked at her door. In this sentence, the word SUSPECTED means   26.____

    A. answered   B. called
    C. distrusted   D. welcomed

27. The aide was POSITIVE that the child hit her. In this sentence, the word POSITIVE means   27.____

    A. annoyed   B. certain   C. sorry   D. surprised

28. The tenant DECLINED to call the Health Department. In this sentence, the word DECLINED means   28.____

    A. agreed   B. decided   C. refused   D. wanted

29. The aide ARRIVED on time.
In this sentence, the word ARRIVED means   29.____

    A. awoke   B. came   C. left   D. delayed

30. The salesman had to DELIVER books to each person he visited.
In this sentence, the word DELIVER means   30.____

    A. give   B. lend   C. mail   D. sell

KEY (CORRECT ANSWERS)

1.	A	11.	A	21.	B
2.	B	12.	D	22.	B
3.	C	13.	C	23.	A
4.	C	14.	B	24.	C
5.	A	15.	D	25.	D
6.	C	16.	A	26.	C
7.	D	17.	C	27.	B
8.	B	18.	B	28.	C
9.	A	19.	A	29.	B
10.	B	20.	D	30.	A

TEST 2

DIRECTIONS: Each question or incomplete statement is followed by several suggested answers or completions. Select the one that BEST answers the question or completes the statement. *PRINT THE LETTER OF THE CORRECT ANSWER IN THE SPACE AT THE RIGHT.*

Questions 1-10.

DIRECTIONS: In Questions 1 through 10, pick the word that means MOST NEARLY the OPPOSITE of the capitalize word in the sentence.

1. It is possible to CONSTRUCT a rat-proof home. The opposite of CONSTRUCT is   1.___

    A. build   B. erect   C. plant   D. wreck

2. The pest control aide had to REPAIR the flat tire. The opposite of the word REPAIR is   2.___

    A. destroy   B. fix   C. mend   D. patch

3. The pest control aide tried to SHOUT the answer. The opposite of the word SHOUT is   3.___

    A. scream   B. shriek   C. whisper   D. yell

4. Daily VISITS are the best.
The opposite of the word VISITS is   4.___

    A. absences   B. exercises   C. lessons   D. trials

5. It is important to ARRIVE early in the morning. The opposite of the word ARRIVE is   5.___

    A. climb   B. descend   C. enter   D. leave

6. Jorge is a group LEADER.
The opposite of the word LEADER is   6.___

    A. boss   B. chief   C. follower   D. overseer

7. The EXTERIOR of the house needs painting.
The opposite of the word EXTERIOR is   7.___

    A. inside   B. outdoors   C. outside   D. surface

8. He CONCEDED the victory.
The opposite of the word CONCEDED is   8.___

    A. admitted   B. denied   C. granted   D. reported

9. He watched the team BEGIN.
The opposite of the word BEGIN is   9.___

    A. end   B. fail   C. gather   D. win

10. Your handwriting is ILLEGIBLE.
The opposite of the word ILLEGIBLE is   10.___

    A. clear   B. confused   C. jumbled   D. unclear

Questions 11-15.

DIRECTIONS: Questions 11 through 15 are to be answered by following the instructions given in each question. Note that 5 possible answers have been given for these questions ONLY. Therefore, for these questions, your choice may be A, B, C, D, or E. .

11. Add:
$$12\frac{1}{2}$$
$$2\frac{1}{4}$$
$$3\frac{1}{4}$$

11._____

The CORRECT answer is

A.   17   B.   174   C.   174   D.   17 3/4   E.   18

12. Subtract: 150

12._____

-80

The CORRECT answer is

A.   70   B.   80   C.   130   D.   150   E.   230

13. After cleaning up some lots in the East Bronx, five cleanup crews loaded the following amounts of garbage on trucks:
Crew No. 1 loaded 2 1/4 tons
Crew No. 2 loaded 3 tons
Crew No. 3 loaded 1 1/4 tons
Crew No. 4 loaded 2 1/4 tons
Crew No. 5 loaded 1/2 ton
The TOTAL number of tons of garbage loaded was

13._____

A.   8   B.   8 1/4   C.   8 3/4   D.   9   E.   9 1/4

14. Subtract: 17 3/4

14._____

- 7 1/4

The CORRECT answer is

A.   7 1/2   B.   10 1/2   C.   14 1/4   D.   17 3/4   E.   25

15. Yesterday, Tom and Bill each received 10 leaflets about rat control. Each supermarket in the neighborhood was supposed to receive one of these leaflets. When the day was over, Tom had 8 leaflets left. Bill had no leaflets left. How many supermarkets got leaflets yesterday?

15._____

A.   8   B.   10   C.   12   D.   18   E.   20

Questions 16-20.

DIRECTIONS: Questions 16 through 20 are to be answered ONLY on the basis of the information in the following statement and chart, DAILY WORK REPORT FORM (Chart A).

Assume that you are a member of the Pest Control Truck Crew Number 1. Julio Rivera is your Crew Chief. The crew is supposed to report to work at nine o'clock in the morning, Since you are the first to show up, at ten minutes before nine, on 5/24 Rivera asks you to help him out by filling in the Daily Work Report Form for him. Driver Hal Williams shows up at nine, and Driver Rick Smith shows up ten minutes after Williams.

DAILY WORK REPORT FORM (Chart A)

Block #1 Crew No.	Block #2 Date	
Block #3 TRUCKS IN USE Truck # _____ # _____ # _____ # _____ # _____ # _____ # _____ # _____ # _____ # _____	Block #4 DRIVER'S NAME _____ _____ _____ _____ _____ _____ _____ _____	Block #5 TIME OF ARRIVAL A.M. P.M.
Block #6 TRUCKS OUT OF ORDER # _____ # _____ # _____ # _____ #	Block #7 ADDRESS OF CLEAN-UP SITE No._____ Street_____	Block #8 Borough Block #9 Signature of Crew Chief

16. According to the above statement, the entry that belongs in Block #9 is

    A. Julio Rivera   B. June Stevens
    C. Jim Watson   D. Hal Williams

16.___

17. According to the above statement, the entry that should be made in Block #2 is

    A. 9:00 A.M.   B. 9:10 P.M.   C. 5/24   D. 7/24

17.___

18. The names of Hal Williams and Rick Smith should appear in Block #

    A. 4   B. 6   C. 7   D. 9

18.___

19. Rick Smith's time of arrival should be entered in Block #5 as _____ A.M.   19._____

    A. 8:50   B. 8:55   C. 9:00   D. 9:10

20. According to the statement, the entry that should be made in Block #1 is   20._____

    A. zero   B. one   C. 5/24   D. 6/24

Questions 21-23.

DIRECTIONS: Questions 21 through 23 are to be answered on the basis of the statement shown below. Use DAILY WORK REPORT FORM (Chart A) on Page 3 as a guide.

   Pete Marberg showed up at a quarter after nine, in the morning, but his truck, No. 22632441, was in the garage for repairs. Steve Marino showed up a half hour after Pete. He was assigned truck No. 6342003, which was in working order.

21. According to the above statement, truck No. 22632441 should be entered in Block #   21._____

    A. 3   B. 4   C. 6   D. 8

22. According to the above statement, Steve Marino showed up at   22._____

    A. 9:00 A.M.   B. 9:15 A.M.   C. 9:30 P.M.   D. 9:45 A.M.

23. According to the above statement, Steve Marino's truck number belongs in Block #3. The number entered there should be   23._____

    A. 22632441   B. 6342003   C. 6432003   D. 26232441

Questions 24-30.

DIRECTIONS: Questions 24 through 30 are to be answered ONLY on basis of the information in the statements above ea question and the following chart, DAILY GARBAGE COLLECTION REPORT (Chart B).

DAILY GARBAGE COLLECTION REPORT C Chart B)				
Block #1	Block #2	Block #3	Block #4	Block #5
No. of Trucks Used For Collection	Address of Garbage Pick-Up	Amount of Garbage Collected	Amount of Garbage Unloaded	Hours During Which Garbage Was Unloaded
#456	45 Southwest	1/2 ton	1/2 ton	From 7 AM To 8 AM
		Block #6	Block #7	Block #8
TOTALS _____		otal Amount of Garbage Collected By All Trucks	Total Amount of Garbage Unloaded By All Trucks	Total Amount of Time Spent Unloading Of All Trucks

24. Truck # 2437752 started unloading garbage at ten
o'clock Monday morning and finished unloading its
garbage that afternoon. The clock looked like this
when the job was done.
The time entries that should be recorded in Block
#5 are
   A. 10 A.M. and 12:15 P.M.
   B. 10 P.M. and 12:30 A.M.
   C. 10 P.M. and 12:00 A.M.
   D. 10 A.M. and 3:00 P.M.

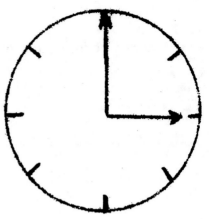

24.

25. Truck # 8967432 had to pick up a load of garbage from 911 South Avenue. It took the
crew until 11:00 A.M. to load the garbage.
According to this statement, the item 911 South Avenue should be entered in Block #

   A. 1   B. 2   C. 3   D. 4

25.

26. On Tuesday, truck # 124356 unloaded 4 ton of garbage, truck # 2437752 unloaded J ton
of garbage, and truck # 435126 unloaded 1/2 ton of garbage.
The TOTAL amount of garbage unloaded by the three trucks on Tuesday should be
entered in Block #

   A. 3   B. 4   C. 5   D. 8

26.

27. On Wednesday, it took truck # 4050607 from 2 P.M. to 6 P.M. to unload 1 ton of garbage.
It took truck # 7040650 from 1 P.M. to 2 P.M. to unload 1/4 ton of garbage. These were
the only trucks working that day.
The TOTAL amount of time it took for both trucks to unload garbage was _____
hours.

   A. 5   B. 6   C. 7   D. 8

27.

28. The amount of garbage collected by one truck should be entered in the DAILY GAR-
BAGE COLLECTION REPORT FORM in Block #

   A. 3   B. 6   C. 7   D. 8

28.

29. Truck # 557799010 reported to 1020 Hudson River Alley to pick up garbage from an
empty lot.
This information should be entered in the DAILY GARBAGE COLLECTION REPORT
FORM in Block # _____ and Block # _____ .

   A. 1; 4   B. 2; 5   C. 1; 2   D. 2; 3

29.

30. It took the Pest Control Truck crew from 8 in the morning to 12 noon to unload the garbage it collected the night before.
This information should be entered in the DAILY GARBAGE COLLECTION REPORT FORM under Block #

30.____

    A. 4   B. 5   C. 6   D. 7

_____

KEY (CORRECT ANSWERS)

1.	D	11.	E	21.	C
2.	A	12.	A	22.	D
3.	C	13.	E	23.	B
4.	A	14.	B	24.	D
5.	D	15.	C	25.	B
6.	C	16.	A	26.	B
7.	A	17.	C	27.	A
8.	B	18.	A	28.	A
9.	A	19.	D	29.	C
10.	A	20.	B	30.	B

_____

EXAMINATION SECTION
TEST 1

DIRECTIONS: Each question or incomplete statement is followed by several suggested answers or completions. Select the one that BEST answers the question or completes the statement. *PRINT THE LETTER OF THE CORRECT ANSWER IN THE SPACE AT THE RIGHT.*

1. Assume that you have been assigned to inspect a building reported to be infested by rats and to prepare a written report thereon.
   Of the following items covered in the report, the LEAST important one is *probably* the

    1.____

    A. fact that rats appear to be feeding on the garbage of a luncheonette which adjoins the building
   B. name and address of the building owner
   C. record of past violations by the owner
   D. statement made by tenants regarding the presence of rats

2. After completing an inspection of a food manufacturing plant, you submit a report of your findings to your supervisor. A few days later, you receive a memorandum from your supervisor indicating that the head of the bureau found your report inadequate. You are to re-inspect the establishment immediately. Your supervisor's memorandum lists the areas which he feels your report did not cover adequately. You, however, are convinced that your report is adequate.
   The BEST course of action for you to take at this time is to

    2.____

    A. refrain from re-inspecting the food establishment unless directed to do so personally by the head of the bureau
   B. re-inspect the premises, submit another report, and then discuss the matter with your supervisor
   C. telephone your supervisor and insist that the matter be fully discussed before you proceed further with a re-inspection
   D. write a letter to the head of the bureau explaining why you feel your report was adequate, and wait for a reply before you re-inspect

3. Assume that you have a close relative who is engaged in the practice of accounting. Following your inspection of a restaurant which is not in violation of the health code, you inform the owner that your relative is an accountant. You hand the owner the accountant's business card and suggest that your relative be considered for any accounting work needed. The owner then tells you that he would like to have your relative take over his accounting work.
   Your action in securing the restaurant's accounting work for your relative is

    3.____

    A. *improper;* you should have discussed the matter with the restaurant owner after your regular working hours
   B. *improper;* you should not have suggested your relative for the owner's accounting work
   C. *proper* as long as the owner remains in full compliance with the health code
   D. *proper* provided that your relative does not discuss the owner's business with you

4. A tenant of an apartment house telephones the department of health to complain that no heat is being furnished to her apartment. The complaint is referred to you with instructions to make a field visit. When you arrive at the apartment house, the tenant partly opens her door but refuses to allow you to enter the apartment. You explain the situation to the tenant, but she persists in her refusal to allow you to enter the apartment.
The BEST thing for you to do in these circumstances is to

    4.

   A. notify the tenant that if she refuses you admittance to her apartment, you may be required to obtain a court order directing her to allow you to enter
   B. place the complaint in your pending file and return to the apartment the next time you are in the neighborhood
   C. prepare a report setting forth that the tenant refused to allow you to enter the apartment
   D. take a reading of the temperature in the hallway and then estimate the temperature in the apartment

5. In the course of your inspection of a luncheonette, you note a violation of a provision of the health code relating to the unsanitary condition of food containers. You point out the condition to the owner as you begin to prepare a notice of violation. The owner becomes very angry and declares that the food containers are clean. To illustrate his point, he shows the food containers to two patrons seated at the lunch counter. Both patrons declare that the food containers are clean and suggest that you not *pick* on the owner. The owner then tells you that if you make trouble for him, he will make trouble for you.
Of the following, the BEST course of action for you to take is to

    5.

   A. inform the owner that you will return at a later date to complete your notice of violation
   B. refrain from giving the owner a notice of violation since he has witnesses to support his position
   C. serve the owner with a notice of violation
   D. telephone your supervisor, tell him of the condition of the food containers, and ask him whether you should give the owner a notice of violation

6. A provision of the health code requires food handlers to take a course in food handling sanitation. Your supervisor requests that when you visit food establishments in your district, you remind them of the code requirement. Your supervisor stresses that your visit is to be an educational one and that you are not to emphasize the mandatory aspect of this provision. Later, you visit a restaurant owner in your district who expresses strong reservations as to the practicability of releasing food handlers to take such a course.
The one statement which you should NOT make to the owner under any circumstances is that if his food handlers take such a course,

    6.

   A. future violations of the health code by the owner will receive special treatment since he is cooperating with the department
   B. his profits may rise since patrons prefer to eat in a place where food sanitation standards are high
   C. the possibility of food poisoning with attendant possible economic loss to the owner will be decreased
   D. the requirement of the health code is mandatory in this respect and must be complied with

7. During your inspection of a multiple dwelling, you find a serious violation of a provision of   7.____
the health code. The owner claims that at one time the particular provision in question
was sensible, but circumstances have changed and the provision should now be
repealed. After listening to the owner, you are convinced that the health code should be
changed as indicated by the owner. The CORRECT course of action for you to take is to

    A.   give the owner a notice of violation and refrain from making any report to your
office concerning the provision in question
    B.   give the owner a notice of violation and suggest to your superior that the provision
be reviewed as to its continued usefulness
    C.   refrain from giving the owner a notice of violation since the provision is obviously
outdated
    D.   refrain from giving the owner a notice of violation until the courts rule on the consti-
tutionality of the provision

8. Assume that you are in the apartment of a tenant who has complained that the landlord   8.____
is not furnishing sufficient heat. Your thermometer shows that the landlord is furnishing
sufficient heat to comply with the pertinent provision of the health code. You so inform the
tenant. The tenant excitedly declares that you are using a *fake* thermometer and that you
may be on the landlord's *payroll.*
Under these circumstances, you should state that

    A.   if the tenant has any allegation to make concerning your inspection or character,
she should contact your department
    B.   if these, allegations are repeated, you will refer the tenant for psychiatric examina-
tion
    C.   the allegations constitute defamation of the character of a public officer, and that
you will so notify the police department
    D.   you will ask the landlord to speak to the tenant to vouch for your honesty

9. You have been assigned to investigate a complaint with regard to a certain fruit and veg-   9.____
etable stand. Your investigation does not disclose any violation. Upon informing the
owner of the stand of your findings, he offers you a bag of fruit as a gift. You decline it. He
then offers to sell you the bag of fruit below the retail price - at cost to him. You SHOULD

    A.   accept the offer, but refrain from visiting the establishment again
    B.   accept the offer, provided you are satisfied that the fruit is being sold to you at cost
    C.   decline the offer because it is not possible to calculate the wholesale cost of the
fruit
    D.   decline the offer since acceptance would be improper

10. The term *FT/SEC* is a unit of   10.____

    A. density   B. length   C. mass   D. speed

11. A container can hold 100 pounds of water or 70 pounds of an *unknown* liquid.   11.____
The specific gravity of the *unknown* liquid is

    A. .30   B. .70   C. 1.0   D. 1.4

12. A *calorie* may be defined as the amount of heat required to raise one   12.____

    A. gram of water 1° C   B. gram of water 1° F
    C. pound of water 1° C   D. pound of water 1° F

13. The acidity of vinegar is due to the presence of _____ acid.   13._

    A. acetic   B. carbonic   C. citric   D. hydrochloric

14. The cleansing action of a soap solution is due PRIMARILY to its   14._

    A. acid reaction   B. increased surface tension
    C. neutral reaction   D. reduced surface tension

15. Titration refers to a process of   15._

    A. determining the normality of an acid solution
    B. determining the refractive index of a crystal
    C. extracting oxygen from water
    D. measuring the quantity of salt present in a saline solution

16. Which one of the following types of compounds ALWAYS includes carbon, hydrogen, and   16._
oxygen?

    A. Carbohydrates   B. Carbonates
    C. Hydrates   D. Hydrocarbons

17. The formula for nitric acid is   17._

    A. HNO_2 B. HNO_3 C. NO_2 D. N_2O

18. Gastric juice owes its acidity, *for the most part,* to the presence of _____ acid.   18._

    A. carbonic   B. hydrochloric   C. nitric   D. sulfuric

19. Insulin is a type of   19._

    A. enzyme   B. hormone   C. sugar   D. vitamin

20. The organ which prevents food from entering the windpipe during the act of swallowing is   20._
the

    A. epiglottis   B. larynx   C. pharynx   D. trachea

21. Casein is a type of   21._

    A. carbohydrate   B. enzyme   C. fat   D. protein

22. The MAIN function of the kidneys is to remove wastes formed as a result of the oxidation   22._
of

    A. carbohydrates B. fats   C. proteins   D. vitamins

23. Vitamin C is ALSO known as _____ acid.   23._

    A. ascorbic   B. citric   C. glutamic   D. lactic

24. Light passes through the crystalline lens in the eye and focuses on the   24._

    A. cornea   B. iris   C. pupil   D. retina

25. An electron weighs   25.____

    A.   less than a neutron   B.   more than a neutron
    C.   the same as a neutron   D.   the same as a proton

KEY (CORRECT ANSWERS)

1.	C	11.	B
2.	B	12.	A
3.	B	13.	A
4.	C	14.	D
5.	C	15.	A
6.	A	16.	A
7.	B	17.	B
8.	A	18.	B
9.	D	19.	B
10.	D	20.	A

21.	D
22.	C
23.	A
24.	D
25.	A

TEST 2

DIRECTIONS: Each question or incomplete statement is followed by several suggested answers or completions. Select the one that BEST answers the question or completes the statement. *PRINT THE LETTER OF THE CORRECT ANSWER IN THE SPACE AT THE RIGHT.*

1. An electron has a _____ charge.   1._

    A. negative   B. positive   C. variable   D. zero

2. Isotopes are atoms of elements which have _____ atomic weight(s).   2._

    A. different atomic numbers and different
    B. different atomic numbers but the same
    C. the same atomic number and the same
    D. the same atomic number but different

3. In the Einstein equation $E = mc^2$, E, m, and c^2 stand for, respectively,   3._

    A. electrons, molecules, and (centimeters)^2
    B. energy, mass, and (light velocity)^2
    C. energy, mass, and (radioactivity)^2
    D. energy, molecules, and (light velocity)^2

4. Photosynthesis entails the absorption of   4._

    A. carbon dioxide and oxygen and release of water
    B. carbon dioxide and water and release of oxygen
    C. oxygen and release of carbon dioxide and water
    D. water and release of carbon dioxide and oxygen

5. Ordinary body temperature is approximately 37 on the _____ scale.   5._

    A. absolute   B. A.P.I.   C. centigrade   D. Fahrenheit

6. Bacteria are _____ chlorphyll.   6._

    A. multicellular organisms containing
    B. multicellular organisms that do not contain
    C. unicellular organisms containing
    D. unicellular organisms that do not contain

7. The immunity acquired as a result of an injection of tetanus antitoxin is termed _____ 7._
immunity.

    A. artificially acquired active
    B. artificially acquired passive
    C. naturally acquired active
    D. naturally acquired passive

8. A virus is the causative agent of   8._

    A. diphtheria   B. smallpox   C. syphilis   D. tuberculosis

9. Typhus fever epidemics are caused by   9.____

    A.   bacteria   B.   rickettsiae   C.   viruses   D.   yeasts

10. The one of the following tests used to determine susceptibility to scarlet fever is the   10.____
    _____ test.

    A.   Dick   B.   Schick   C.   Wasserman   D.   Widal

11. Generally, the type of individual immunity to disease which is of the LONGEST duration   11.____
    is brought about by

    A.   antibody production stimulated by killed microorganisms
    B.   antibody production stimulated by live microorganisms
    C.   transfer of antibodies during pregnancy from an immune mother to her unborn
        child by placental transfer
    D.   transfer of antibodies from one adult to another

12. Diabetes is considered to be a(n) _____ disease.   12.____

    A.   communicable   B.   contagious
    C.   noninfectious   D.   infectious

13. The genus *Mycobacterium* contains a species responsible for   13.____

    A.   diphtheria   B.   gonorrhea
    C.   tuberculosis   D.   whooping cough

14. The pH of a neutral solution is   14.____

    A.   3   B.   5   C.   7   D.   9

15. Of the following, the pair that is NOT a set of equivalents is   15.____

    A.   .014% .00014   B.   1/5% .002
    C.   1.5% 3/200   D.   115% .115

16. 10^{-2} is equal to   16.____

    A.   0.001   B.   0.01   C.   0.1   D.   100.0

17. $10^2 \times 10^3$ is equal to   17.____

    A. 10^5 B. 10^6 C. 100^5 D. 100^6

18. The length of two objects are in the ratio of 2:1. If each were 3 inches shorter, the ratio   18.____
    would be 3:1. The longer object is _____ inches.

    A.   8   B.   10   C.   12   D.   14

19. If the weight of water is 62.4 pounds per cubic foot, the weight of the water that fills a   19.____
    rectangular container 6 inches by 6 inches by 1 foot is _____ pounds.

    A.   7.8   B.   15.6   C.   31.2   D.   46.8

20. *Dry-ice* is solid   20.____

    A.   ammonia   B.   carbon dioxide
    C.   freon   D.   sulfur dioxide

21. The fat content of normal milk is *approximately*   21.___

    A. 1%   B. 4%   C. 10%   D. 16%

22. The one of the following acids GENERALLY responsible for the natural souring of milk is   22.___
    _____ acid.

    A. acetic   B. amino   C. citric   D. lactic

23. From a nutritional standpoint, milk is *deficient* in   23.___

    A. iron   B. lactose
    C. mineral salts   D. protein

24. The man who is USUALLY known as the father of chemotherapy is   24.___

    A. Paul Ehrlich   B. Elie Metchnikoff
    C. Louis Pasteur   D. John Tyndall

25. The success of this country in building the Panama Canal was due to the successful con-   25.___
    quest of yellow fever.
    The man who directed the study which led to this conquest was

    A. Joseph Lister   B. Walter Reed
    C. Theobold Smith   D. William Welch

———

KEY (CORRECT ANSWERS)

1.	A		11.	B
2.	D		12.	C
3.	B		13.	C
4.	B		14.	C
5.	C		15.	D
6.	D		16.	B
7.	B		17.	A
8.	B		18.	C
9.	B		19.	B
10.	A		20.	B

21.	B
22.	D
23.	A
24.	A
25.	B

———

TEST 3

DIRECTIONS: Each question or incomplete statement is followed by several suggested answers or completions. Select the one that BEST answers the question or completes the statement. *PRINT THE LETTER OF THE CORRECT ANSWER IN THE SPACE AT THE RIGHT.*

1. The *Babcock test* is used in milk analysis to determine _____ content.

   A. butterfat   B. mineral   C. protein   D. vitamin

   1._____

2. The phosphatase test is used to determine whether milk

   A. has an objectionable odor
   B. has been adequately pasteurized
   C. has been adulterated
   D. is too alkaline

   2._____

3. A lactometer is used in milk inspection work to determine the

   A. acidity of milk   B. color of milk
   C. percentage of milk solids   D. specific gravity of milk

   3._____

4. Milk samples collected at milk plants should be taken from milk cans, the contents of which have

   A. not been stirred so that sediment does not appear in the sample
   B. not been stirred so that the growth of bacteria which thrive on oxygen is not encouraged
   C. been stirred in order to obtain a representative sample
   D. been stirred so that the percentage of dissolved oxygen meets required standards

   4._____

5. In the holding process, milk should be pasteurized for at least 30 minutes at a temperature of about

   A. 115° F   B. 145° F   C. 180° F   D. 212° F

   5._____

6. Undulant fever, which may be contracted from milk, is caused by an organism known as

   A. Bacillus subtilis   B. Brucella abortus
   C. Staphylococcus aureus   D. Streptococcus pyogenes

   6._____

7. The presence of *milk stone* or *water stone* in dairy equipment is

   A. *desirable;* it indicates that dairy equipment is modern
   B. *desirable;* it indicates that milking machines have been sterilized
   C. *undesirable;* it will increase the bacterial count of milk that comes in contact with it
   D. *undesirable;* it will greatly increase the percentage of water in the final milk product

   7._____

8. The type of dairy barn flooring which is LEAST desirable from a sanitarian's point of view is

   A. asphalt   B. compressed cork and asphalt
   C. concrete   D. wood

   8._____

9. *Curds* and *whey* are substances encountered in the manufacture of cheese. Of the two substances, usually one

   9._____

A. is made into cheese; the other is a by-product used to feed animals
B. is made into cheese; the other is made into butter
C. is made into hard cheese; the other is made into soft cheese
D. refers to bacteria-ripened cheese; the other refers to mold-ripened cheese

10. Botulism food poisoning in the United States is USUALLY caused by

A. eating fish caught in polluted waters
B. failure to wash raw fruit before eating
C. improper home-canning of fruits and vegetables
D. tapeworms found in beef or sheep

11. The growth of pathogenic bacteria in preserved dates and figs is *inhibited* because these foods have a high _____ content.

A. acid   B. mineral   C. protein   D. sugar

12. In the heating of the following foods during canning, the one which generally requires the LOWEST temperature to prevent microbiological activity is

A. fish   B. fruit   C. meat   D. milk

13. Food poisoning cases in the United States are USUALLY characterized by _____ followed by death.

A. long periods of illness
B. long periods of illness rarely
C. short periods of illness
D. short periods of illness rarely

14. In the United States, food poisoning due to eating mushrooms is LARGELY attributable to

A. failure to cook mushrooms
B. failure to wash mushrooms
C. mushrooms which are blue in color
D. mushrooms which have not been cultivated domestically

15. Of the following, the food whose flavor is NOT improved by the addition of monosodium glutamate is

A. cooked vegetables   B. fruit juice
C. meats   D. seafood and chowders

16. A NEW method of food preservation involves preservation by

A. chemicals   B. drying   C. heat   D. radiation

17. In grading meat, the term *finish* refers to

A. distribution of fat   B. muscle hardness
C. presence of tapeworm   D. symmetry of the carcass

18. Of the following preservatives, the one which may NOT be legally used in the preservation of meat is

    A. benzoic acid   B. salt
    C. sugar   D. wood smoke

18.____

19. A vitamin known to be effective in the prevention of pellagra is

    A. ascorbic acid   B. niacin
    C. riboflavin   D. thiamin

19.____

20. Eggs are *candled* for the purpose of determining

    A. calcium content
    B. size of the egg
    C. the presence of blood spots
    D. weight of the egg

20.____

———

KEY (CORRECT ANSWERS)

1.	A	11.	D
2.	B	12.	B
3.	D	13.	D
4.	C	14.	D
5.	B	15.	B
6.	B	16.	D
7.	C	17.	A
8.	D	18.	A
9.	A	19.	B
10.	C	20.	C

———

TEST 4

DIRECTIONS: Each question or incomplete statement is followed by several suggested answers or completions. Select the one that BEST answers the question or completes the statement. *PRINT THE LETTER OF THE CORRECT ANSWER IN THE SPACE AT THE RIGHT.*

1. Foodstuffs such as cereal and flour do not readily spoil as a result of bacterial action because such foodstuffs usually have a low _____ content.   1._

   A. acid   B. ash   C. sodium   D. water

2. The presence of bacteria responsible for typhoid fever in a public water supply is PROBABLY traceable to   2._

   A. fecal contamination
   B. excessive water aeration
   C. pus from skin lesions
   D. rotting animal and fish remains

3. Objectionable tastes and odors in public water supplies are, in the great majority of cases, due to the presence of   3._

   A. algae and protozoa   B. animal remains
   C. dissolved oxygen   D. yeasts and molds

4. Atmospheric pressure as indicated by the mercury barometer at sea level is GENERALLY about _____ inches.   4._

   A. 10   B. 15   C. 30   D. 45

5. The CHIEF objective of a sewage treatment and disposal system is to   5._

   A. alter sewage by chemical treatment so that it may be sold as commercial fertilizer
   B. convert liquid sludge so that it may be used as drinking water
   C. convert sewage into a form usable as land fill
   D. remove or decompose the organic matter

6. *Warfarin* is GENERALLY used in the control of   6._

   A. ants   B. flies   C. lice   D. rats

7. The control of the common housefly has been regarded as important because houseflies   7._

   A. are a great nuisance although they are not responsible for the transmission of diseases
   B. may transmit diseases by biting humans
   C. may transmit diseases by contaminating food with pathogenic organisms
   D. may transmit diseases by injecting pathogenic organisms into the bloodstream of animals which are later eaten by man

8. The term *Anopheles* refers to a type of   8._

   A. ant   B. louse   C. mosquito   D. termite

9. Galvanized iron is made by coating iron with

    A. chromium   B. lead   C. tin   D. zinc

9.____

10. The amount of oxygen in the air of a properly ventilated room, expressed as a percentage of volume, is APPROXIMATELY

    A. 5%   B. 10%   C. 15%   D. 20%

10.____

11. Field control of hay fever generally depends upon the effective use of a(n)

    A. bacteriostatic agent   B. fungicide
    C. insect spray   D. weed killer

11.____

12. An orthotolidine testing set may be used to determine the presence of

    A. bacterial growth in milk cans and pails
    B. chlorine in wash and rinse waters
    C. DDT dust in foods such as flour and sugar
    D. organisms responsible for the spoilage of shucked oysters

12.____

13. The one of the following which is NOT a characteristic of carbon monoxide gas is that it

    A. causes nausea and vomiting
    B. has a strong irritating odor
    C. interferes with the oxygen-carrying power of the blood
    D. is a common constituent of manufactured gas

13.____

Question 14.

DIRECTIONS: Question 14 is based on the following statement.

The rise of science is the most important fact of modern life. No student should be permitted to complete his education without understanding it. From a scientific education, we may expect an understanding of science. From scientific investigation, we may expect scientific knowledge. We are confusing the issue and demanding what we have no right to ask if we seek to learn from science the goals of human life and of organized society.

14. The foregoing statement implies MOST NEARLY that

14.____

    A. in a democratic society, the student must determine whether to pursue a scientific education
    B. organized society must learn from science how to meet the needs of modern life
    C. science is of great value in molding the character and values of the student
    D. scientific education is likely to lead the student to acquire an understanding of scientific processes

Questions 15-16.

DIRECTIONS: Questions 15 and 16 are based on the following statement.

Since sewage is a variable mixture of substances from many sources, it is to be expected that its microbial flora will fluctuate both in types and numbers. Raw sewage may contain millions of bacteria per milliliter. Prominent among these are the coliforms. strepto-

cocci, anaerobic spore forming bacilli, the Proteus group, and other types which have their origin in the intestinal tract of man. Sewage is also a potential source of pathogenic intestinal organisms. The poliomyelitis virus has been demonstrated to occur in sewage; other viruses are readily isolated from the same source. Aside from the examination of sewage to demonstrate the presence of some specific microorganism for epidemiological purposes, bacteriological analysis provides little useful information because of the magnitude of variations known to occur with regard to both numbers and kinds.

15. According to the above passage,   15._

    A. all sewage contains pathogenic organisms
    B. bacteriological analysis of sewage is routinely performed in order to determine the presence of coliform organisms
    C. microorganisms found in sewage vary from time to time
    D. poliomyelitis epidemics are due to viruses found in sewage

16. The title which would be MOST suitable for the above passage is: 16._

    A. Disposal of Sewage by Bacteria
    B. Microbes and Sewage Treatment
    C. Microbiological Characteristics of Sewage
    D. Sewage Removal Processes

Questions 17-18.

DIRECTIONS: Questions 17 and 18 are based on the following statement.

Most cities carrying on public health work exercise varying degrees of inspection and control over their milk supplies. In some cases, it consists only of ordinances, with little or no attempt at enforcement. In other cases, good control is obtained through wise ordinances and an efficient inspecting force and laboratory. While inspection alone can do much toward controlling the quality and production of milk, there must also be frequent laboratory tests of the milk.

The bacterial count of the milk indicates the condition of the dairy and the methods of milk handling. The counts, therefore, are a check on the reports of the sanitarian. High bacterial counts of milk from a dairy reported by a sanitarian to be "good" may indicate difficulty not suspected by the sanitarian such as infected udders, inefficient sterilisation of utensils, or poor cooling.

17. According to the above passage, the MOST accurate of the following statements is: 17._

    A. The bacterial count of milk will be low if milk-producing animals are free from disease.
    B. A high bacterial count of milk can be reduced by pasteurization.
    C. The bacterial count of milk can be controlled by the laboratory.
    D. The bacterial count of milk will be low if the conditions of milk production, processing and handling are good.

18. The following conclusion may be drawn from the above passage: 18._____

    A. Large centers of urban population usually exercise complete control over their milk supplies.

    B. Adequate legislation is an important adjunct of a milk supply control program.

    C. Most cities should request the assistance of other cities prior to instituting a milk supply control program.

    D. Wise laws establishing a milk supply control program obviate the need for the enforcement of such laws provided that good laboratory techniques are employed.

Question 19-20.

DIRECTIONS: Questions 19 and 20 are based upon the following excerpt from the health code.

Article 101 Shellfish and Fish
Section 101. 03 Shippers of shellfish; registration

    (a)   No shellfish shall be shipped into the city unless the shipper of such shellfish is registered with the department.

    (b)   Application for registration shall be made on a form furnished by the department.

    (c)   The following shippers shall be eligible to apply for registration :

       1. A shipper of shellfish located in the state but outside the city who holds a shellfish shipper's permit issued by the state conservation department; or

       2. A shipper of shellfish located outside the state, or located in Canada, who holds a shellfish certificate of approval or a permit issued by the state or provincial agency having control of the shellfish industry of his state or province, which certificate of approval or permit appears on the current list of interstate shellfish shipper permits published by the United States Public Health Service.

    (d)   The commissioner may refuse to accept the registration of any applicant whose past observance of the shellfish regulations is not satisfactory to the commissioner.

    (e)   No applicant shall ship shellfish into the city unless he has been notified in writing by the department that his application for registration has been approved.

    (f)   Every registration as a shipper of shellfish, unless sooner revoked, shall terminate on the expiration date of the registrant's state shellfish certificate or permit.

19. The above excerpt from the health code provides that   19._____

    A. permission to register may not be denied to a shellfish shipper meeting the standards of his own jurisdiction

    B. permission to register will not be denied unless the shipper's past observances of shellfish regulations has not been satisfactory to the U.S. Public Health Service

    C. the commissioner may suspend the regulations applicable to registration if requested to do so by the governmental agency having jurisdiction over the shellfish shipper

    D. an applicant for registration as a shellfish shipper may ship shellfish into the city when notified by the department in writing that his application has been approved

20. The above excerpt from the health code provides that   20.__

   A. applications for registration will not be granted to out-of-state shippers of shellfish who have already received permission to sell shellfish from another jurisdiction
   B. shippers of shellfish located outside of the city may not ship shellfish into the city unless the shellfish have passed inspection by the jurisdiction in which the shellfish shipper is located
   C. a shipper of shellfish located in Canada is eligible for registration provided that he holds a shellfish permit issued by the appropriate provincial agency and that such permit appears on the current list of shellfish shipper permits published by the U.S. Public Health Service
   D. a shipper of shellfish located in Canada whose shellfish permit has been revoked by the provincial agency may ship shellfish into the city until such time as he is notified in writing by the department that his shellfish registration has been revoked

---

KEY (CORRECT ANSWERS)

1.	D		11.	D
2.	A		12.	B
3.	A		13.	B
4.	C		14.	D
5.	D		15.	C
6.	D		16.	C
7.	C		17.	D
8.	C		18.	B
9.	D		19.	D
10.	D		20.	C

PREPARING WRITTEN MATERIAL

PARAGRAPH REARRANGEMENT
COMMENTARY

The sentences which follow are in scrambled order. You are to rearrange them in proper order and indicate the letter choice containing the correct answer at the space at the right.

Each group of sentences in this section is actually a paragraph presented in scrambled order. Each sentence in the group has a place in that paragraph; no sentence is to be left out. You are to read each group of sentences and decide upon the best order in which to put the sentences so as to form as well-organized paragraph.

The questions in this section measure the ability to solve a problem when all the facts relevant to its solution are not given.

More specifically, certain positions of responsibility and authority require the employee to discover connections between events sometimes, apparently, unrelated. In order to do this, the employee will find it necessary to correctly infer that unspecified events have probably occurred or are likely to occur. This ability becomes especially important when action must be taken on incomplete information.

Accordingly, these questions require competitors to choose among several suggested alternatives, each of which presents a different sequential arrangement of the events. Competitors must choose the MOST logical of the suggested sequences.

In order to do so, they may be required to draw on general knowledge to infer missing concepts or events that are essential to sequencing the given events. Competitors should be careful to infer only what is essential to the sequence. The plausibility of the wrong alternatives will always require the inclusion of unlikely events or of additional chains of events which are NOT essential to sequencing the given events.

It's very important to remember that you are looking for the best of the four possible choices, and that the best choice of all may not even be one of the answers you're given to choose from.

There is no one right way to these problems. Many people have found it helpful to first write out the order of the sentences, as they would have arranged them, on their scrap paper before looking at the possible answers. If their optimum answer is there, this can save them some time. If it isn't, this method can still give insight into solving the problem. Others find it most helpful to just go through each of the possible choices, contrasting each as they go along. You should use whatever method feels comfortable, and works, for you.

While most of these types of questions are not that difficult, we've added a higher percentage of the difficult type, just to give you more practice. Usually there are only one or two questions on this section that contain such subtle distinctions that you're unable to answer confidently, and you then may find yourself stuck deciding between two possible choices, neither of which you're sure about.

Preparing Written Material

EXAMINATION SECTION
TEST 1

DIRECTIONS: The following groups of sentences need to be arranged in an order that makes sense. Select the letter preceding the sequence that represents the best sentence order. *PRINT THE LETTER OF THE CORRECT ANSWER IN THE SPACE AT THE RIGHT.*

Question 1

1.____

1. The ostrich egg shell's legendary toughness makes it an excellent substitute for certain types of dishes or dinnerware, and in parts of Africa ostrich shells are cut and decorated for use as containers for water.
2. Since prehistoric times, people have used the enormous egg of the ostrich as a part of their diet, a practice which has required much patience and hard work-to hard-boil an ostrich egg takes about four hours.
3. Opening the egg's shell, which is rock hard and nearly an inch thick, requires heavy tools, such as a saw or chisel; from inside, a baby ostrich must use a hornlike projection on its beak as a miniature pick-axe to escape from the egg.
4. The offspring of all higher-order animals originate from single egg cells that are carried by mothers, and most of these eggs are relatively small, often microscopic.
5. The egg of the African ostrich, however, weighs a massive thirty pounds, making it the largest single cell on earth, and a common object of human curiosity and wonder.

The best order is

A. 5 4 1 2 3
B. 1 4 5 3 2
C. 4 2 3 5 1
D. 4 5 2 3 1

Question 2

2.____

1. Typically only a few feet high on the open sea, individual tsunami have been known to circle the entire globe two or three times if their progress is not interrupted, but are not usually dangerous until they approach the shallow water that surrounds land masses.
2. Some of the most terrifying and damaging hazards caused by earthquakes are tsunami, which were once called "tidal waves"— a poorly chosen name, since these waves have nothing to do with tides.
3. Then a wave, slowed by the sudden drag on the lower part of its moving water column, will pile upon itself, sometimes reaching a height of over 100 feet.
4. Tsunami (Japanese for "great harbor wave") are seismic waves that are caused by earthquakes near oceanic trenches, and once triggered, can travel up to 600 miles an hour on the open ocean.
5. A land-shoaling tsunami is capable of extraordinary destruction; some tsunami have deposited large boats miles inland, washed out two-foot-thick seawalls, and scattered locomotive trains over long distances.

The best order is

A. 4 1 3 2 5
B. 1 3 4 2 5
C. 5 1 3 2 4
D. 2 4 1 3 5

Question 3

1. Soon, by the 1940's, jazz was the most popular type of music among American intellectuals and college students.
2. In the early days of jazz, it was considered "lowdown" music, or music that was played only in rough, disreputable bars and taverns.
3. However, jazz didn't take long to develop from early ragtime melodies into more complex, sophisticated forms, such as Charlie Parker's "bebop" style of jazz.
4. After charismatic band leaders such as Duke Ellington and Count Basic brought jazz to a larger audience, and jazz continued to evolve into more complicated forms, white audiences began to accept and even to enjoy the new American art form.
5. Many white Americans, who then dictated the tastes of society, were wary of music that was played almost exclusively in black clubs in the poorer sections of cities and towns.

The best order is

A. 5 4 3 2 1
B. 2 5 3 4 1
C. 4 5 3 1 2
D. 1 2 4 3 5

Question 4

1. Then, hanging in a windless place, the magnetized end of the needle would always point to the south.
2. The needle could then be balanced on the rim of a cup, or the edge of a fingernail, but this balancing act was hard to maintain, and the needle often fell off.
3. Other needles would point to the north, and it was important for any traveler finding his way with a compass to remember which kind of magnetized needle he was carrying.
4. To make some of the earliest compasses in recorded history, ancient Chinese "magicians" would rub a needle with a piece of magnetized iron called a lodestone.
5. A more effective method of keeping the needle free to swing with its magnetic pull was to attach a strand of silk to the center of the needle with a tiny piece of wax.

The best order is

A. 4 2 5 1 3
B. 4 3 5 2 1
C. 4 5 2 1 3
D. 4 1 3 5 2

Question 5

5.____

1. The now-famous first mate of the *HMS Bounty,* Fletcher Christian, founded one of the world's most peculiar civilizations in 1790.
2. The men knew they had just committed a crime for which they could be hanged, so they set sail for Pitcairn, a remote, abandoned island in the far eastern region of the Polynesian archipelago, accompanied by twelve Polynesian women and six men.
3. In a mutiny that has become legendary, Christian and the others forced Captain Bligh into a lifeboat and set him adrift off the coast of Tonga in April of 1789.
4. In early 1790, the *Bounty* landed at Pitcairn Island, where the men lived out the rest of their lives and founded an isolated community which to this day includes direct descendants of Christian and the other crewmen.
5. The *Bounty,* commanded by Captain William Bligh, was in the middle of a global voyage, and Christian and his shipmates had come to the conclusion that Bligh was a reckless madman who would lead them to their deaths unless they took the ship from him.

The best order is

A.   4 5 3 2 1
B.   1 3 5 2 4
C.   1 5 3 2 4
D.   3 1 5 4 2

Question 6

6.____

1. But once the vines had been led to make orchids, the flowers had to be carefully hand-pollinated, because unpollinated orchids usually lasted less than a day, wilting and dropping off the vine before it had even become dark.
2. The Totonac farmers discovered that looping a vine back around once it reached a five-foot height on its host tree would cause the vine to flower.
3. Though they knew how to process the fruit pods and extract vanilla's flavoring agent, the Totonacs also knew that a wild vanilla vine did not produce abundant flowers or fruit.
4. Wild vines climbed along the trunks and canopies of trees, and this constant upward growth diverted most of the vine's energy to making leaves instead of the orchid flowers that, once pollinated, would produce the flavorful pods.
5. Hundreds of years before vanilla became a prized food flavoring in Europe and the Western World, the Totonac Indians of the Mexican Gulf Coast were skilled cultivators of the vanilla vine, whose fruit they literally worshipped as a goddess.

The best order is

A.   2 3 4 1 5
B.   2 4 3 1 5
C.   5 3 4 2 1
D.   3 4 1 2 5

Question 7   7.

1. Once airborne, the spider is at the mercy of the air currents—usually the spider takes a brief journey, traveling close to the ground, but some have been found in air samples collected as high as 10,000 feet, or been reported landing on ships far out at sea.
2. Once a young spider has hatched, it must leave the environment into which it was born as quickly as possible, in order to avoid competing with its hundreds of brothers and sisters for food.
3. The silk rises into warm air currents, and as soon as the pull feels adequate the spider lets go and drifts up into the air, suspended from the silk strand in the same way that a person might parasail.
4. To help young spiders do this, many species have adapted a practice known as "aerial dispersal," or, in common speech, "ballooning."
5. A spider that wants to leave its surroundings quickly will climb to the top of a grass stem or twig, face into the wind, and aim its back end into the air, releasing a long stream of silk from the glands near the tip of its abdomen.

The best order is

A. 5 4 2 3 1
B. 5 2 4 1 3
C. 2 5 4 3 1
D. 2 4 5 3 1

Question 8   8.

1. For about a year, Tycho worked at a castle in Prague with a scientist named Johannes Kepler, but their association was cut short by another argument that drove Kepler out of the castle, to later develop, on his own, the theory of planetary orbits.
2. Tycho found life without a nose embarrassing, so he made a new nose for himself out of silver, which reportedly remained glued to his face for the rest of his life.
3. Tycho Brahe, the 17th-century Danish astronomer, is today more famous for his odd and arrogant personality than for any contribution he has made to our knowledge of the stars and planets.
4. Early in his career, as a student at Rostock University, Tycho got into an argument with the another student about who was the better mathematician, and the two became so angry that the argument turned into a sword fight, during which Tycho's nose was sliced off.
5. Later in his life, Tycho's arrogance may have kept him from playing a part in one of the greatest astronomical discoveries in history: the elliptical orbits of the solar system's planets.

The best order is

A. 1 4 2 3 5
B. 4 2 3 5 1
C. 4 2 1 3 5
D. 3 4 2 5 1

Question 9

9.____

1. The processionaries are so used to this routine that if a person picks up the end of a silk line and brings it back to the origin—creating a closed circle—the caterpillars may travel around and around for days, sometimes starving ar freezing, without changing course.
2. Rather than relying on sight or sound, the other caterpillars, who are lined up end-to-end behind the leader, travel to and from their nests by walking on this silk line, and each will reinforce it by laying down its own marking line as it passes over.
3. In order to insure the safety of individuals, the processionary caterpillar nests in a tree with dozens of other caterpillars, and at night, when it is safest, they all leave together in search of food.
4. The processionary caterpillar of the European continent is a perfect illustration of how much some insect species rely on instinct in their daily routines.
5. As they leave their nests, the processionaries form a single-file line behind a leader who spins and lays out a silk line to mark the chosen path.

The best order is

A. 4 3 5 2 1
B. 3 5 4 2 1
C. 3 5 2 1 4
D. 4 5 3 1 2

Question 10

10.____

1. Often, the child is also given a handcrafted walker or push cart, to provide support for its first upright explorations.
2. In traditional Indian families, a child's first steps are celebrated as a ceremonial event, rooted in ancient myth.
3. These carts are often intricately designed to resemble the chariot of Krishna, an important figure in Indian mythology.
4. The sound of these anklet bells is intended to mimic the footsteps of the legendary child Rama, who is celebrated in devotional songs throughout India.
5. When the child's parents see that the child is ready to begin walking, they will fit it with specially designed ankle bracelets, adorned with gently ringing bells.

The best order is

A. 2 3 4 1 5
B. 2 5 3 1 4
C. 5 4 1 3 2
D. 5 3 2 1 4

Question 11

1. The settlers planted Osage orange all across Middle America, and today long lines and rectangles of Osage orange trees can still be seen on the prairies, running along the former boundaries of farms that no longer exist.
2. After trying sod walls and water-filled ditches with no success, American farmers began to look for a plant that was adaptable to prairie weather, and that could be trimmed into a hedge that was "pig-tight, horse-high, and bull-strong."
3. The tree, so named because it bore a large (but inedible) fruit the size of an orange, was among the sturdiest and hardiest of American trees, and was prized among Native Americans for the strength and flexibility of bows which were made from its wood.
4. The first people to practice agriculture on the American flatlands were faced with an important problem: what would they use to fence their land in a place that was almost entirely without trees or rocks?
5. Finally, an Illinois farmer brought the settlers a tree that was native to the land between the Red and Arkansas rivers, a tree called the Osage orange.

The best order is

 A. 2 1 5 3 4
 B. 1 2 3 4 5
 C. 4 2 5 3 1
 D. 4 2 1 3 5

Question 12

1. After about ten minutes of such spirited and complicated activity, the head dancer is free to make up his or her own movements while maintaining the interest of the New Year's crowd.
2. The dancer will then perform a series of leg kicks, while at the same time operating the lion's mouth with his own hand and moving the ears and eyes by means of a string which is attached to the dancer's own mouth.
3. The most difficult role of this dance belongs to the one who controls the lion's head; this person must lead all the other "parts" of the lion through the choreographed segments of the dance.
4. The head dancer begins with a complex series of steps, alternately stepping forward with the head raised, and then retreating a few steps while lowering the head, a movement that is intended to create the impression that the lion is keeping a watchful eye for anything evil.
5. When performing a traditional Chinese New Year's lion dance, several performers must fit themselves inside a large lion costume and work together to enact different parts of the dance.

The best order is

 A. 5 3 4 2 1
 B. 3 4 2 5 1
 C. 3 1 5 4 2
 D. 4 2 3 5 1

Question 13   13._____

1. For many years the shell of the chambered nautilus was treasured in Europe for its beauty and intricacy, but collectors were unaware that they were in possession of the structure that marked a "missing link" in the evolution of marine mollusks.
2. The nautilus, however, evolved a series of enclosed chambers in its shell, and invented a new use for the structure: the shell began to serve as a buoyancy device.
3. Equipped with this new flotation device, the nautilus did not need the single, muscular foot of its predecessors, but instead developed flaps, tentacles, and a gentle form of jet propulsion that transformed it into the first mollusk able to take command of its own destiny and explore a three-dimensional world.
4. By pumping and adjusting air pressure into the chambers, the nautilus could spend the day resting on the bottom, and then rise toward the surface at night in search of food.
5. The nautilus shell looks like a large snail shell, similar to those of its ancestors, who used their shells as protective coverings while they were anchored to the sea floor.

The best order is

A. 5 2 4 1 3
B. 5 1 2 3 4
C. 1 2 5 3 4
D. 1 5 2 4 3

Question 14   14._____

1. While France and England battled for control of the region, the Acadiens prospered on the fertile farmland, which was finally secured by England in 1713.
2. Early in the 17th century, settlers from western France founded a colony called Acadie in what is now the Canadian province of Nova Scotia.
3. At this time, English officials feared the presence of spies among the Acadiens who might be loyal to their French homeland, and the Acadiens were deported to spots along the Atlantic and Caribbean shores of America.
4. The French settlers remained on this land, under English rule, for around forty years, until the beginning of the French and Indian War, another conflict between France and England.
5. As the Acadien refugees drifted toward a final home in southern Louisiana, neighbors shortened their name to "Cadien," and finally "Cajun," the name which the descendants of early Acadiens still call themselves.

The best order is

A. 1 4 2 3 5
B. 2 1 3 5 4
C. 2 1 4 3 5
D. 5 2 3 4 1

Question 15   15.

    1.   Traditional households in the Eastern and Western regions of Africa serve two meals a day-one at around noon, and the other in the evening.

    2.   The starch is then used in the way that Americans might use a spoon, to scoop up a portion of the main dish on the person's plate.

    3.   The reason for the starch's inclusion in every meal has to do with taste as well as nutrition; African food can be very spicy, and the starch is known to cool the burning effect of the main dish.

    4.   When serving these meals, the main dish is usually served on individual plates, and the starch is served on a communal plate, from which diners break off a piece of bread or scoop rice or fufu in their fingers.

    5.   The typical meals usually consist of a thick stew or soup as the main course, and an accompanying starch—either bread, rice, *or fufu, a* starchy grain paste similar in consistency to mashed potatoes.

The best order is

    A.   5 2 3 4 1
    B.   5 1 4 3 2
    C.   1 4 5 3 2
    D.   1 5 4 2 3

Question 16   16.

    1.   In the early days of the American Midwest, Indiana settlers sometimes came together to hold an event called an apple peeling, where neighboring settlers gathered at the home-stead of a host family to help prepare the hosts' apple crop for cooking, canning, and mak-ing apple butter.

    2.   At the beginning of the event, each peeler sat down in front of a ten- or twenty-gallon stone jar and was given a crock of apples and a paring knife.

    3.   Once a peeler had finished with a crock, another was placed next to him; if the peeler was an unmarried man, he kept a strict count of the number of apples he had peeled, because the winner was allowed to kiss the girl of his choice.

    4.   The peeling usually ended by 9:30 in the evening, when the neighbors gathered in the host family's parlor for a dance social.

    5.   The apples were peeled, cored, and quartered, and then placed into the jar.

The best order is

    A.   1 5 3 4 2
    B.   2 5 3 4 1
    C.   1 2 5 3 4
    D.   2 1 5 4 3

Question 17

17._____

1. If your pet turtle is a land turtle and is native to temperate climates, it will stop eating some time in October, which should be your cue to prepare the turtle for hibernation.
2. The box should then be covered with a wire screen, which will protect the turtle from any rodents or predators that might want to take advantage of a motionless and helpless animal.
3. When your turtle hasn't eaten for a while and appears ready to hibernate, it should be moved to its winter quarters, most likely a cellar or garage, where the temperature should range between 40° and 45° F.
4. Instead of feeding the turtle, you should bathe it every day in warm water, to encourage the turtle to empty its intestines in preparation for its long winter sleep.
5. Here the turtle should be placed in a well-ventilated box whose bottom is covered with a moisture-absorbing layer of clay beads, and then filled three-fourths full with almost dry peat moss or wood chips, into which the turtle will burrow and sleep for several months.

The best order is

A. 1 4 3 5 2
B. 3 4 2 5 1
C. 3 2 4 1 5
D. 4 5 2 3 1

Question 18

18._____

1. Once he has reached the nest, the hunter uses two sturdy bamboo poles like huge chopsticks to pull the nest away from the mountainside, into a large basket that will be lowered to people waiting below.
2. The world's largest honeybees colonize the Nepalese mountainsides, building honeycombs as large as a person on sheer rock faces that are often hundreds of feet high.
3. In the remote mountain country of Nepal, a small band of "honey hunters" carry out a tradition so ancient that 10,000 year-old drawings of the practice have been found in the caves of Nepal.
4. To harvest the honey and beeswax from these combs, a honey hunter climbs above the nests, lowers a long bamboo-fiber ladder over the cliff, and then climbs down.
5. Throughout this dangerous practice, the hunter is stung repeatedly, and only the veterans, with skin that has been toughened over the years, are able to return from a hunt without the painful swelling caused by stings.

The best order is

A. 2 4 3 5 1
B. 2 4 1 5 3
C. 5 3 2 4 1
D. 3 2 4 1 5

Question 19

19

1. After the Romans left Britain, there were relentless attacks on the islands from the barbarian tribes of northern Germany—the Angles, Saxons, and Jutes.
2. As the empire weakened, Roman soldiers withdrew from Britain, leaving behind a country that continued to practice the Christian religion that had been introduced by the Romans.
3. Early Latin writings tell of a Christian warrior named Arturius (Arthur, in English) who led the British citizens to defeat these barbarian invaders, and brought an extended period of peace to the lands of Britain.
4. Long ago, the British Isles were part of the far-flung Roman Empire that extended across most of Europe and into Africa and Asia.
5. The romantic legend of King Arthur and his knights of the Round Table, one of the most popular and widespread stories of all time, appears to have some foundation in history.

The best order is

A. 5 4 3 2 1
B. 5 4 2 1 3
C. 4 5 2 3 1
D. 4 3 2 1 5

Question 20

20.

1. The cylinder was allowed to cool until it sould stand on its own, and then it was cut from the tube and split down the side with a single straight cut.
2. Nineteenth-century glassmakers, who had not yet discovered the glazier's modern techniques for making panes of glass, had to create a method for converting their blown glass into flat sheets.
3. The bubble was then pierced at the end to make a hole that opened up while the glassmaker gently spun it, creating a cylinder of glass.
4. Turned on its side and laid on a conveyor belt, the cylinder was strengthened, or tempered, by being heated again and cooled very slowly, eventually flattening out into a single rectangular piece of glass.
5. To do this, the glassmaker dipped the end of a long tube into melted glass and blew into the other end of the tube, creating an expanding bubble of glass.

The best order is

A. 2 5 3 4 1
B. 2 4 5 3 1
C. 3 5 2 4 1
D. 3 1 4 5 2

Question 21   21.____

1. The splints are almost always hidden, but horses are occasionally born whose splinted toes project from the leg on either side, just above the hoof.
2. The second and fourth toes remained, but shrank to thin splints of bone that fused invisibly to the horse's leg bone.
3. Horses are unique among mammals, having evolved feet that each end in what is essentially a single toe, capped by a large, sturdy hoof.
4. Julius Caesar, an emperor of ancient Rome, was said to have owned one of these three-toed horses, and considered it so special that he would not permit anyone else to ride it.
5. Though the horse's earlier ancestors possessed the traditional mammalian set of five toes on each foot, the horse has retained only its third toe; its first and fifth toes disappeared completely as the horse evolved.

The best order is

A. 3 5 2 1 4
B. 5 3 2 4 1
C. 3 2 5 1 4
D. 5 2 3 1 4

Question 22   22.____

1. The new building materials—some of which are twenty feet long, and weigh nearly six tons—were transported to Pohnpei on rafts, and were brought into their present position by using hibiscus fiber ropes and leverage to move the stone columns upward along the inclined trunks of coconut palm trees.
2. The ancestors built great fires to heat the stone, and then poured cool seawater on the columns, which caused the stone to contract and split along natural fracture lines.
3. The now-abandoned enclave of Nan Madol, a group of 92 man-made islands off the shore of the Micronesian island of Pohnpei, is estimated to have been built around the year 500 A.D.
4. The islanders say their ancestors quarried stone columns from a nearby island, where large basalt columns were formed by the cooling of molten lava.
5. The structures of Nan Madol are remarkable for the sheer size of some of the stone "logs" or columns that were used to create the walls of the offshore community, and today anthropologists can only rely on the information of existing local people for clues about how Nan Madol was built.

The best order is

A. 5 4 3 2 1
B. 5 3 1 4 2
C. 3 5 4 2 1
D. 3 1 4 2 5

Question 23

1. One of the most easily manipulated substances on earth, glass can be made into ceramic tiles that are composed of over 90% air.
2. NASA's space shuttles are the first spacecraft ever designed to leave and re-enter the earth's atmosphere while remaining intact.
3. These ceramic tiles are such effective insulators that when a tile emerges from the oven in which it was fired, it can be held safely in a person's hand by the edges while its interior still glows at a temperature well over 2000° F.
4. Eventually, the engineers were led to a material that is as old as our most ancient civiliza-tionsglass.
5. Because the temperature during atmospheric re-entry is so incredibly hot, it took NASA's engineers some time to find a substance capable of protecting the shuttles.

The best order is

A. 5 2 1 3 4
B. 2 5 4 1 3
C. 2 3 1 2 5
D. 5 4 3 1 2

Question 24

1. The secret to teaching any parakeet to talk is patience, and the understanding that when a bird "talks," it is simply imitating what it hears, rather than putting ideas into words.
2. You should stay just out of sight of the bird and repeat the phrase you want it to learn, for at least fifteen minutes every morning and evening.
3. It is important to leave the bird without any-words of encouragement or farewell; otherwise it might combine stray remarks or phrases, such as "Good night," with the phrase you are trying to teach it.
4. For this reason, to train your bird to imitate your words you should keep it free of any dis-tractions, especially other noises, while you are giving it "lessons."
5. After your repetition, you should quietly leave the bird alone for a while, to think over what it has just heard.

The best order is

A. 1 4 2 5 3
B. 1 2 4 3 5
C. 3 2 1 5 4
D. 3 1 5 4 2

Question 25   25._____

1. As a school approaches, fishermen from neighboring communities join their fishing boats together as a fleet, and string their gill nets together to make a huge fence that is held up by cork floats.
2. At a signal from the party leaders, or *nakura,* the family members pound the sides of the boats or beat the water with long poles, creating a sudden and deafening noise.
3. The fishermen work together to drag the trap into a half-circle that may reach 300 yards in diameter, and then the families move their boats to form the other half of the circle around the school of fish.
4. The school of fish flee from the commotion into the awaiting trap, where a final wall of net is thrown over the open end of the half-circle, securing the day's haul.
5. Indonesian people from the area around the Sulu islands live on the sea, in floating villages made of lashed-together or stilted homes, and make much of their living by fishing their home waters for migrating schools of snapper, scad, and other fish.

The best order is

A.   1 5 3 4 2
B.   1 2 4 3 5
C.   5 1 2 3 4
D.   5 1 3 2 4

KEY (CORRECT ANSWERS)

1.	D		11.	C
2.	D		12.	A
3.	B		13.	D
4.	A		14.	C
5.	C		15.	D
6.	C		16.	C
7.	D		17.	A
8.	D		18.	D
9.	A		19.	B
10.	B		20.	A

21. A
22. C
23. B
24. A
25. D

PREPARING WRITTEN MATERIALS

EXAMINATION SECTION
TEST 1

DIRECTIONS: Each of the following questions consists of a sentence which may be classified appropriately under one of the following four categories:
  A.   Incorrect because of faulty grammar or sentence structure
  B.   Incorrect because of faulty punctuation
  C.   Incorrect because of faulty spelling or capitalization
  D.   Correct

Examine each sentence carefully. Then, in the space at the right, print the letter preceding the best of the four alternatives suggested above. All incorrect sentences contain but one type of error. Consider a sentence correct if it contains none of the types of errors mentioned, even though there may be other correct ways of expressing the same thought.

1.   The fire apparently started in the storeroom, which is usually locked.   1._____

2.   On approaching the victim two bruises were noticed by this officer.   2._____

3.   The officer, who was there examined the report with great care.   3._____

4.   Each employee in the office had a separate desk.   4._____

5.   Each employee in the office had a separate desk.   5._____

6.   The suggested procedure is similar to the one now in use.   6._____

7.   No one was more pleased with the new procedure than the chauffeur.   7._____

8.   He tried to pursuade her to change the procedure.   8._____

9.   The total of the expenses charged to petty cash were high.   9._____

10.   An understanding between him and I was finally reached.   10._____

11.   It was at the supervisor's request that the clerk agreed to postpone his vacation.   11._____

12.   We do not believe that it is necessary for both he and the clerk to attend the conference.   12._____

13.   All employees, who display perseverance, will be given adequate recognition.   13._____

14.   He regrets that some of us employees are dissatisfied with our new assignments.   14._____

15.   "Do you think that the raise was merited," asked the supervisor?   15._____

16.   The new manual of procedure is a valuable supplament to our rules and regulation.   16._____

17.   The typist admitted that she had attempted to pursuade the other employees to assist her in her work.   17._____

18. The supervisor asked that all amendments to the regulations be handled by you and I. 18._

19. They told both he and I that the prisoner had escaped. 19._

20. Any superior officer, who, disregards the just complaints of his subordinates, is remiss in the performance of his duty. 20._

21. Only those members of the national organization who resided in the Middle west attended the conference in Chicago. 21._

22. We told him to give the investigation assignment to whoever was available. 22._

23. Please do not disappoint and embarass us by not appearing in court. 23._

24. Despite the efforts of the Supervising mechanic, the elevator could not be started. 24._

25. The U.S. Weather Bureau, weather record for the accident date was checked. 25._

KEY (CORRECT ANSWERS)

1.	D		11.	D
2.	A		12.	A
3.	B		13.	B
4.	D		14.	D
5.	B		15.	B
6.	C		16.	C
7.	D		17.	C
8.	C		18.	A
9.	A		19.	A
10.	A		20.	B

21.	C
22.	D
23.	C
24.	C
25.	B

TEST 2

DIRECTIONS: Each question consists of a sentence. Some of the sentences contain errors in English grammar or usage, punctuation, spelling, or capitalization. A sentence does not contain an error simply because it could be written in a different manner. Choose answer
    A. If the sentence contains an error in English grammar or usage
    B. If the sentence contains an error in punctuation
    C. If the sentence contains an error in spelling or capitalization
    D. If the sentence does not contain any errors.

1. The severity of the sentence prescribed by contemporary statutes - including both the former and the revised New York Penal Laws - do not depend on what crime was intended by the offender.

    1._____

2. It is generally recognized that two defects in the early law of attempt played a part in the birth of burglary: (1) immunity from prosecution for conduct short of the last act before completion of the crime, and (2) the relatively minor penalty imposed for an attempt (it being a common law misdemeanor) vis-a-vis the completed offense.

    2._____

3. The first sentence of the statute is applicable to employees who enter their place of employment, invited guests, and all other persons who have an express or implied license or privilege to enter the premises.

    3._____

4. Contemporary criminal codes in the United States generally divide burglary into various degrees, differentiating the categories according to place, time and other attendent circumstances.

    4._____

5. The assignment was completed in record time but the payroll for it has not yet been preparid.

    5._____

6. The operator, on the other hand, is willing to learn me how to use the mimeograph.

    6._____

7. She is the prettiest of the three sisters.

    7._____

8. She doesn't know; if the mail has arrived.

    8._____

9. The doorknob of the office door is broke.

    9._____

10. Although the department's supply of scratch pads and stationery have diminished considerably, the allotment for our division has not been reduced.

    10._____

11. You have not told us whom you wish to designate as your secretary.

    11._____

12. Upon reading the minutes of the last meeting, the new proposal was taken up for consideration.

    12._____

13. Before beginning the discussion, we locked the door as a precautionery measure.

    13._____

14. The supervisor remarked, "Only those clerks, who perform routine work, are permitted to take a rest period."

    14._____

15. Not only will this duplicating machine make accurate copies, but it will also produce a quantity of work equal to fifteen transcribing typists.

    15._____

16. "Mr. Jones," said the supervisor, "we regret our inability to grant you an extent ion of your leave of absence."   16._

17. Although the employees find the work monotonous and fatigueing, they rarely complain.   17._

18. We completed the tabulation of the receipts on time despite the fact that Miss Smith our fastest operator was absent for over a week.   18._

19. The reaction of the employees who attended the meeting, as well as the reaction of those who did not attend, indicates clearly that the schedule is satisfactory to everyone concerned.   19._

20. Of the two employees, the one in our office is the most efficient.   20._

21. No one can apply or even understand, the new rules and regulations.   21._

22. A large amount of supplies were stored in the empty office.   22._

23. If an employee is occassionally asked to work overtime, he should do so willingly.   23._

24. It is true that the new procedures are difficult to use but, we are certain that you will learn them quickly.   24._

25. The office manager said that he did not know who would be given a large allotment under the new plan.   25._

KEY (CORRECT ANSWERS)

1.	A		11.	D
2.	D		12.	A
3.	D		13.	C
4.	C		14.	B
5.	C		15.	A
6.	A		16.	C
7.	D		17.	C
8.	B		18.	B
9.	A		19.	D
10.	A		20.	A

21.	B
22.	A
23.	C
24.	B
25.	D

TEST 3

DIRECTIONS: Each of the following sentences may be classified MOST appropriately under one of the following our categories:
  A. faulty because of incorrect grammar;
  B. faulty because of incorrect punctuation;
  C. faulty because of incorrect capitalization;
  D. correct

Examine each sentence carefully. Then, in the space at the right, print the capital letter preceding the option which is the BEST of the four suggested above. All incorrect sentences contain but one type of error. Consider a sentence correct if it contains none of the types of errors mentioned, even though there may be other correct ways of expressing the same thought.

1. The desk, as well as the chairs, were moved out of the office.   1.____

2. The clerk whose production was greatest for the month won a day's vacation as first prize.   2.____

3. Upon entering the room, the employees were found hard at work at their desks.   3.____

4. John Smith our new employee always arrives at work on time.   4.____

5. Punish whoever is guilty of stealing the money.   5.____

6. Intelligent and persistent effort lead to success no matter what the job may be.   6.____

7. The secretary asked, "can you call again at three o'clock?"   7.____

8. He told us, that if the report was not accepted at the next meeting, it would have to be rewritten.   8.____

9. He would not have sent the letter if he had known that it would cause so much excitement.   9.____

10. We all looked forward to him coming to visit us.   10.____

11. If you find that you are unable to complete the assignment please notify me as soon as possible.   11.____

12. Every girl in the office went home on time but me; there was still some work for me to finish.   12.____

13. He wanted to know who the letter was addressed to, Mr. Brown or Mr. Smith.   13.____

14. "Mr. Jones, he said, please answer this letter as soon as possible."   14.____

15. The new clerk had an unusual accent inasmuch as he was born and educated in the south.   15.____

16. Although he is younger than her, he earns a higher salary.   16.____

17. Neither of the two administrators are going to attend the conference being held in Wash-   17.__
    ington, D.C.

18. Since Miss Smith and Miss Jones have more experience than us, they have been given   18.__
    more responsible duties.

19. Mr. Shaw the supervisor of the stock room maintains an inventory of stationery and office   19.__
    supplies.

20. Inasmuch as this matter affects both you and I, we should take joint action.   20.__

21. Who do you think will be able to perform this highly technical work?   21.__

22. Of the two employees, John is considered the most competent.   22.__

23. He is not coming home on tuesday; we expect him next week.   23.__

24. Stenographers, as well as typists must be able to type rapidly and accurately.   24.__

25. Having been placed in the safe we were sure that the money would not be stolen.   25.__

KEY (CORRECT ANSWERS)

1.	A	11.	B
2.	D	12.	D
3.	A	13.	A
4.	B	14.	B
5.	D	15.	C
6.	A	16.	A
7.	C	17.	A
8.	A	18.	A
9.	D	19.	B
10.	A	20.	A

21.	D
22.	A
23.	C
24.	B
25.	A

TEST 4

DIRECTIONS: Each of the following sentences consist of four sentences lettered A, B, C, and D. One of the sentences in each group contains an error in grammar or punctuation. Indicate the INCORRECT sentence in each group. *PRINT THE LETTER OF THE CORRECT ANSWER IN THE SPACE AT THE RIGHT.*

1. A. Give the message to whoever is on duty.   1.____
    B. The teacher who's pupil won first prize presented the award.
    C. Between you and me, I don't expect the program to succeed.
    D. His running to catch the bus caused the accident.

2. A. The process, which was patented only last year is already obsolete.   2.____
    B. His interest in science (which continues to the present) led him to convert his basement into a laboratory.
    C. He described the book as "verbose, repetitious, and bombastic".
    D. Our new director will need to possess three qualities: vision, patience, and fortitude.

3. A. The length of ladder trucks varies considerably.   3.____
    B. The probationary fireman reported to the officer to whom he was assigned.
    C. The lecturer emphasized the need for we firemen to be punctual.
    D. Neither the officers nor the members of the company knew about the new procedure.

4. A. Ham and eggs is the specialty of the house.   4.____
    B. He is one of the students who are on probation.
    C. Do you think that either one of us have a chance to be nominated for president of the class?
    D. I assume that either he was to be in charge or you were.

5. A. Its a long road that has no turn.   5.____
    B. To run is more tiring than to walk.
    C. We have been assigned three new reports: namely, the statistical summary, the narrative summary, and the budgetary summary.
    D. Had the first payment been made in January, the second would be due in April.

6. A. Each employer has his own responsibilities.   6.____
    B. If a person speaks correctly, they make a good impression.
    C. Every one of the operators has had her vacation.
    D. Has anybody filed his report?

7. A. The manager, with all his salesmen, was obliged to go.   7.____
    B. Who besides them is to sign the agreement?
    C. One report without the others is incomplete.
    D. Several clerks, as well as the proprietor, was injured.

8. A. A suspension of these activities is expected.   8.____
    B. The machine is economical because first cost and upkeep are low.
    C. A knowledge of stenography and filing are required for this position.
    D. The condition in which the goods were received shows that the packing was not done properly.

9.   A.   There seems to be a great many reasons for disagreement.   9.__
      B.   It does not seem possible that they could have failed.
      C.   Have there always been too few applicants for these positions?
      D.   There is no excuse for these errors.

10.   A.   We shall be pleased to answer your question.   10.__
      B.   Shall we plan the meeting for Saturday?
      C.   I will call you promptly at seven.
      D.   Can I borrow your book after you have read it?

11.   A.   You are as capable as I.   11.__
      B.   Everyone is willing to sign but him and me.
      C.   As for he and his assistant, I cannot praise them too highly.
      D.   Between you and me, I think he will be dismissed.

12.   A.   Our competitors bid above us last week.   12.__
      B.   The survey which was began last year has not yet been completed.
      C.   The operators had shown that they understood their instructions.
      D.   We have never ridden over worse roads.

13.   A.   Who did they say was responsible?   13.__
      B.   Whom did you suspect?
      C.   Who do you suppose it was?
      D.   Whom do you mean?

14.   A.   Of the two propositions, this is the worse.   14.__
      B.   Which report do you consider the best -- the one in January or the one in July?
      C.   I believe this is the most practicable of the many plans submitted.
      D.   He is the youngest employee in the organization.

15.   A.   The firm had but three orders last week.   15.__
      B.   That doesn't really seem possible.
      C.   After twenty years scarcely none of the old business remains.
      D.   Has he done nothing about it?

KEY (CORRECT ANSWERS)

1.	B		6.	B
2.	A		7.	D
3.	C		8.	C
4.	C		9.	A
5.	A		10.	D

11.	C
12.	B
13.	A
14.	B
15.	C

REPORT WRITING

EXAMINATION SECTION
TEST 1

DIRECTIONS: Each question or incomplete statement is followed by several suggested answers or completions. Select the one that *BEST* answers the question or completes the statement. *PRINT THE LETTER OF THE CORRECT ANSWER IN THE SPACE AT THE RIGHT.*

1. Following are six steps that should be taken in the course of report preparation:
    I. Outlining the material for presentation in the report
    II. Analyzing and interpreting the facts
    III. Analyzing the problem
    IV. Reaching conclusions
    V. Writing, revising, and rewriting the final copy
    VI. Collecting data
   According to the principles of good report writing, the CORRECT order in which these steps should be taken is:

   A. VI, III, II, I, IV, V   B. III, VI, II, IV, I, V
   C. III, VI, II, I, IV, V   D. VI, II, III, IV, I, V

1._____

2. Following are three statements concerning written reports:
    I. Clarity is generally more essential in oral reports than in written reports.
    II. Short sentences composed of simple words are generally preferred to complex sentences and difficult words.
    III. Abbreviations may be used whenever they are customary and will not distract the attention of the reader
   Which of the following choices correctly classifies the above statements in to whose which are valid and those which are not valid?

   A. I and II are valid, but III is not valid.
   B. I is valid, but II and III are not valid.
   C. II and III are valid, but I is not valid.
   D. III is valid, but I and II are not valid.

2._____

3. In order to produce a report written in a style that is both understandable and effective, an investigator should apply the principles of unit, coherence, and emphasis. The one of the following which is the BEST example of the principle of coherence is

   A. interlinking sentences so that thoughts flow smoothly
   B. having each sentence express a single idea to facilitate comprehension
   C. arranging important points in prominent positions so they are not overlooked
   D. developing the main idea fully to insure complete consideration

3._____

4. Assume that a supervisor is preparing a report recommending that a standard work procedure be changed. Of the following, the MOST important information that he should include in this report is

   A. a complete description of the present procedure
   B. the details and advantages of the recommended procedure

4._____

A. the type and amount of retraining needed
B. the percentage of men who favor the change

5. When you include in your report on an inspection some information which you have obtained from other individuals, it is *MOST* important that   5._

    A. this information have no bearing on the work these other people are performing
    B. you do not report as fact the opinions of other individuals
    C. you keep the source of the information confidential
    D. you do not tell the other individuals that their statements will be included in your report.

6. Before turning in a report of an investigation of an accident, you discover some additional information you did not know about when you wrote the report.   6._
Whether or not you re-write your report to include this additional information should depend *MAINLY* on the

    A. source of this additional information
    B. established policy covering the subject matter of the report
    C. length of the report and the time it would take you to re-write it
    D. bearing this additional information will have on the conclusions in the report

7. The *most desirable FIRST* step in the planning of a written report is to   7._

    A. ascertain what necessary information is readily available in the files
    B. outline the methods you will employ to get the necessary information
    C. determine the objectives and uses of the report
    D. estimate the time and cost required to complete the report

8. In writing a report, the practice of taking up the *least* important points *first* and the *most* important points *last* is a   8._

    A. *good* technique since the final points made in a report will make the greatest impression on the reader
    B. *good* technique since the material is presented in a more logical manner and will lead directly to the conclusions
    C. *poor* technique since the reader's time is wasted by having to review irrelevant information before finishing the report
    D. *poor* technique since it may cause the reader to lose interest in the report and arrive at incorrect conclusions about the report

9. Which one of the following serves as the *BEST* guideline for you to follow for effective written reports? Keep sentences   9._

    A. *short* and limit sentences to *one* thought
    B. *short* and use *as many* thoughts as possible
    C. *long* and limit sentences to *one* thought
    D. *long* and use *as many* thoughts as possible

10. One method by which a supervisor might prepare written reports to management is to begin with the conclusions, results, or summary, and to follow this with the supporting data.   10._
The *BEST* reason why management may *prefer* this form of report is that

A. management lacks the specific training to understand the data
B. the data completely supports the conclusions
C. time is saved by getting to the conclusions of the report first
D. the data contains all the information that is required for making the conclusions

11. When making written reports, it is MOST important that they be   11._____

     A. well-worded   B. accurate as to the facts
     B. brief   D. submitted immediately

12. Of the following, the MOST important reason for a supervisor to prepare good written   12._____
reports is that

     A. a supervisor is rated on the quality of his reports
     B. decisions are often made on the basis of the reports
     C. such reports take less time for superiors to review
     D. such reports demonstrate efficiency of department operations

13. Of the following, the BEST test of a good report is whether it   13._____

     A. provides the information needed
     B. shows the good sense of the writer
     C. is prepared according to a proper format
     D. is grammatical and neat

14. When a supervisor writes a report, he can BEST show that he has an understanding of   14_____
the subject of the report by

     A. including necessary facts and omitting nonessential details
     B. using statistical data
     C. giving his conclusions but not the data on which they are based
     D. using a technical vocabulary

15. Suppose you and another supervisor on the same level are assigned to work together on   15._____
a report. You disagree strongly with one of the recommendations the other supervisor
wants to   include in the report but you cannot change his views.
Of the following, it would be BEST that

     A. you refuse to accept responsibility for the report
     B. you ask that someone else be assigned to this project to replace you
     C. each of you state his own ideas about this recommendation in the report
     D. you give in to the other supervisor's opinion for the sake of harmony

16. Standardized forms are often provided for submitting reports.   16._____
Of the following, the MOST important advantage of using standardized forms for
reports is that

     A. they take less time to prepare than individually written reports
     B. the person making the report can omit information he considers unimportant
     C. the responsibility for preparing these reports can be turned over to subordinates
     D. necessary information is less likely to be omitted

17. A report which may *BEST* be classed as a *periodic* report is one which   17

    A. requires the same type of information at regular intervals
    B. contains detailed information which is to be retained in permanent records
    C. is prepared whenever a special situation occurs
    D. lists information in graphic form

18. In the writing of reports or letters, the ideas presented in a paragraph are usually of   18.
    unequal importance and require varying degrees of emphasis.
    All of the following are methods of placing extra stress on an idea *EXCEPT*

    A. repeating it in a number of forms
    B. placing it in the middle of the paragraph
    C. placing it either at the beginning or at the end of the paragraph
    D. underlining it

Questions 19-25.

DIRECTIONS: Questions 19 to 25 concern the subject of report writing and are based on the
                information and incidents described in the paragraph below. (In answering
                these questions, assume that the facts and incidents in the paragraph are
                true.)

On December 15, at 8 a.m., seven Laborers reported to Foreman Joseph Meehan in
the Greenbranch Yard in Queens. Meehan instructed the men to load some 50-pound boxes
of books on a truck for delivery to an agency building in Brooklyn. Meehan told the men that,
because the boxes were rather heavy, two men should work together, helping each other lift
and load each box. Since Michael Harper, one of the Laborers, was without a partner, Meehan helped him with the boxes for a while. When Meehan was called to the telephone in a
nearby building, however, Harper decided to lift a box himself. He appeared able to lift the
box, but, as he got the box halfway up, he cried out that he had a sharp pain in his back.
Another Laborer, Jorge Ortiz, who was passing by, ran over to help Harper put the box down.
Harper suddenly dropped the box, which fell on Ortiz' right foot. By this time Meehan had
come out of the building. He immediately helped get the box off Ortiz' foot and had both men
lie down. Meehan covered the men with blankets and called an ambulance, which arrived a
half hour later. At the hospital, the doctor said that the X-ray results showed that Ortiz' right
foot was broken in three places.

19. What would be the *BEST* term to use in a report describing the injury of Jorge Ortiz?   19.

    A. Strain   B. Fracture   C. Hernia   D. Hemorrhage

20. Which of the following would be the MOST accurate summary for the Foreman to put in   20.
    his report of the incident?

    A. Ortiz attempted to help Harper carry a box which was too heavy for one person,
       but Harper dropped it before Ortiz got there.
    B. Ortiz tried to help Harper carry a box but Harper got a pain in his back and acci-
       dentally dropped the box on Ortiz' foot.
    C. Harper refused to follow Meehan's orders and lifted a box too heavy for him; he
       deliberately dropped it when Ortiz tried to help him carry it.
    D. Harper lifted a box and felt a pain in his back; Ortiz tried to help Harper put the
       box down but Harper accidentally dropped it on Ortiz' foot.

21. One of the Laborers at the scene of the accident was asked his version of the incident.   21. ___
Which information obtained from this witness would be *LEAST* important for
including in the accident report?

    A. His opinion as to the cause of the accident
    B. How much of the accident he saw
    C. His personal opinion of the victims
    D. His name and address

22. What should be the *MAIN* objective of writing a report about the incident described in the   22. ___
above paragraph? To

    A. describe the important elements in the accident situation
    B. recommend that such Laborers as Ortiz be advised not to interfere in
        another's work unless given specific instructions
    C. analyze the problems occurring when there are not enough workers to perform
        a certain task
    D. illustrate the hazards involved in performing routine everyday tasks

23. Which of the following is information *missing* from the passage above but which *should*   23. ___
be included in a report of the incident? The

    A. name of the Laborer's immediate supervisor
    B. contents of the boxes
    C. time at which the accident occurred
    D. object or action that caused the injury to Ortiz' foot

24. According to the description of the incident, the accident occurred *because*   24. ___

    A. Ortiz attempted to help Harper who resisted his help
    B. Harper failed to follow instructions given him by Meehan
    C. Meehan was not supervising his men as closely as he should have
    D. Harper was not strong enough to carry the box once he lifted it

25. Which of the following is *MOST* important for a foreman to *avoid* when writing up an offi-   25. ___
cial accident report?

    A. Using technical language to describe equipment involved in the accident
    B. Putting in details which might later be judged unnecessary
    C. Giving an opinion as to conditions that contributed to the accident
    D. Recommending discipline for employees who, in his opinion, caused the accident

KEY (CORRECT ANSWERS)

1.	B		11.	B
2.	C		12.	B
3.	A		13.	A
4.	B		14.	A
5.	B		15.	C
6.	D		16.	D
7.	C		17.	A
8.	D		18.	B
9.	A		19.	B
10.	C		20.	D

21.	C
22.	A
23.	C
24.	B
25.	D

TEST 2

DIRECTIONS: Each question or incomplete statement is followed by several suggested answers or completions. Select the one that *BEST* answers the question or completes the statement. *PRINT THE LETTER OF THE CORRECT ANSWER IN THE SPACE AT THE RIGHT.*

1. Lieutenant X is preparing a report to submit to his commanding officer in order to get approval of a plan of operation he has developed.
The report starts off with the statement of the problem and continues with the details of the problem. It contains factual information gathered with the help of field and operational personnel. It contains a final conclusion and recommendation for action. The recommendation is supplemented by comments from other precinct staff members on how the recommendations will affect their areas of responsibility. The report also includes directives and general orders ready for the commanding officer's signature. In addition, it has two statements of objections presented by two precinct staff members.
Which one of the following, if any, is *either* an item that Lieutenant X should have included in his report and which is not mentioned above, *or* is an item which Lieutenant X improperly did include in his report?

    A. Considerations of alternative courses of action and their consequences should have been covered in the report.
    B. The additions containing documented objections to the recommended course of action should not have been included as part of the report.
    C. A statement on the qualifications of Lieutenant X, which would support his expertness in the field under consideration, should have been included in the report.
    D. The directives and general orders should not have been prepared and included in the report until the commanding officer had approved the recommendations.
    E. None of the above, since Lieutenant X's report was both proper and complete.

1. ____

2. During a visit to a section, the district supervisor criticizes the method being used by the assistant foreman to prepare a certain report and orders him to modify the method. This change ordered by the district supervisor is in direct conflict with the specific orders of the foreman. In this situation, it would be *BEST* for the assistant foreman to

    A. change the method and tell the foreman about the change at the first opportunity
    B. change the method and rely on the district supervisor to notify the foreman
    C. report the matter to the foreman and delay the preparation of the report
    D. ask the district supervisor to discuss the matter with the foreman but use the old method for the time being

2. ____

3. A department officer should realize that the *most usual* reason for writing a report is to

    A. give orders and follow up their execution
    B. establish a permanent record
    C. raise questions
    D. supply information

3. ____

4. A very important report which is being prepared by a department officer will soon be due on the desk of the district supervisor. No typing help is available at this time for the officer. For the officer to write out this report in longhand in such a situation would be

4. ____

A. *bad;* such a report would not make the impression a typed report would
B. *good;* it is important to get the report in on time
C. *bad;* the district supervisor should not be required to read longhand reports
D. *good;* it would call attention to the difficult conditions under which this section must work

5. In a well-written report, the length of each paragraph in the report should be   5.

   A. varied according to the content
   B. not over 300 words
   C. pretty nearly the same
   D. gradually longer as the report is developed and written

6. A clerk in the headquarters office complains to you about the way in which you are filling   6.
out a certain report. It would be *BEST* for you to

   A. tell the clerk that you are following official procedures in filling out the report
   B. ask to be referred to the clerk's superior
   C. ask the clerk exactly what is wrong with the way in which you are filling out the report
   D. tell the clerk that you are following the directions of the district supervisor

7. The use of an outline to help in writing a report is   7.

   A. *desirable* in order to insure good organization and coverage
   B. *necessary* so it can be used as an introduction to the report itself
   C. *undesirable* since it acts as a straight jacket and may result in an unbalanced report
   D. *desirable* if you know your immediate supervisor reads reports with extreme care and attention

8. It is advisable that a department officer do his paper work and report writing as soon as   8.
he has completed an inspection *MAINLY* because

   A. there are usually deadlines to be met
   B. it insures a steady work-flow
   C. he may not have time for this later
   D. the facts are then freshest in his mind

9. Before you turn in a report you have written of an investigation that you have made, you   9.
discover some additional information you didn't know about before. Whether or not you
re-write your report to include this additional information should depend *MAINLY* on the

   A. amount of time remaining before the report is due
   B. established policy of the department covering the subject matter of the report
   C. bearing this information will have on the conclusions of the report
   D. number of people who will eventually review the report

10. When a supervisory officer submits a periodic report to the district supervisor, he should   10.
realize that the *CHIEF* importance of such a report is that it

   A. is the principal method of checking on the efficiency of the supervisor and his sub-
      ordinates
   B. is something to which frequent reference will be made

C. eliminates the need for any personal follow-up or inspection by higher echelons
D. permits the district supervisor to exercise his functions of direction, supervision, and control better

11. Conclusions and recommendations are usually better placed at the *end* rather than at the *beginning* of a report because

    A. the person preparing the report may decide to change some of the conclusions and recommendations before he reaches the end of the report
    B. they are the most important part of the report
    C. they can be judged better by the person to whom the report is sent after he reads the facts and investigations which come earlier in the report
    D. they can be referred to quickly when needed without reading the rest of the report

11.____

12. The use of the same method of record-keeping and reporting by *all* agency sections is

    A. *desirable, MAINLY* because it saves time in section operations
    B. *undesirable, MAINLY* because it kills the initiative of the individual section foreman
    C. *desirable, MAINLY* because it will be easier for the administrator to evaluate and compare section operations
    D. *undesirable, MAINLY* because operations vary from section to section and uniform record-keeping and reporting is not appropriate

12.____

13. The *GREATEST* benefit the section officer will have from keeping complete and accurate records and reports of section operations is that

    A. he will find it easier to run his section efficiently
    B. he will need less equipment
    C. he will need less manpower
    D. the section will run smoothly when he is out

____

14. You have prepared a report to your superior and are ready to send it forward. But on re-reading it, you think some parts are not clearly expressed and your superior may have difficulty getting your point.
Of the following, it would be *BEST* for you to

    A. give the report to one of your men to read, and if he has no trouble understanding it send it through
    B. forward the report and call your superior the next day to ask whether it was all right
    C. forward the report as is; higher echelons should be able to understand any report prepared by a section officer
    D. do the report over, re-writing the sections you are in doubt about

14.____

15. The *BEST* of the following statements concerning reports is that

    A. a carelessly written report may give the reader an impression of inaccuracy
    B. correct grammar and English are unimportant if the main facts are given
    C. every man should be required to submit a daily work report
    D. the longer and more wordy a report is, the better it will read

15.____

16. In writing a report, the question of whether or not to include certain material could be determined *BEST* by considering the

    A. amount of space the material will occupy in the report
    B. amount of time to be spent in gathering the material
    C. date of the material
    D. value of the material to the superior who will read the report

17. Suppose you are submitting a fairly long report to your superior. The *one* of the following sections that should come *FIRST* in this report is a

    A. description of how you gathered material
    B. discussion of possible objections to your recommendations
    C. plan of how your recommendations can be put into practice
    D. statement of the problem dealt with

Questions 18-20.

DIRECTIONS: A foreman is asked to write a report on the incident described in the following passage. Answer Questions 18 through 20 based on the following information

On March 10, Henry Moore, a laborer, was in the process of transferring some equipment from the machine shop to the third floor. He was using a dolly to perform this task and, as he was wheeling the material through the machine shop, laborer Bob Greene called to him. As Henry turned to respond to Bob, he jammed the dolly into Larry Mantell's leg, knocking Larry down in the process and causing the heavy drill that Larry was holding to fall on Larry's foot. Larry started rubbing his foot and then, infuriated, jumped up and punched Henry in the jaw. The force of the blow drove Henry's head back against the wall. Henry did not fight back; he appeared to be dazed. An ambulance was called to take Henry to the hospital, and the ambulance attendant told the foreman that it appeared likely that Henry had suffered a concussion. Larry's injuries consisted of some bruises, but he refused medical attention.

18. An adequate report of the above incident should give as minimum information the names of the persons involved, the names of the witnesses, the date and the time that each event took place, *and* the

    A. names of the ambulance attendants
    B. names of all the employees working in the machine shop
    C. location where the accident occurred
    D. nature of the previous safety training each employee had been given

19. The *only* one of the following which is *NOT* a fact is

    A. Bob called to Henry
    B. Larry suffered a concussion
    C. Larry rubbed his foot
    D. the incident took place in the machine shop

20. Which of the following would be, the MOST accurate summary of the incident for the foreman to put in his report of the accident?   20. ___

    A. Larry Mantell punched Henry Moore because a drill fell on his foot and he was angry. Then Henry fell and suffered a concussion.

    B. Henry Moore accidentally jammed a dolly into Larry Mantell's foot, knocking Larry down. Larry punched Henry, pushing him into the wall and causing him to bang his head against the wall.

    C. Bob Greene called Henry Moore. A dolly then jammed into Larry Mantell and knocked him down. Larry punched Henry who tripped and suffered some bruises. An ambulance was called.

    D. A drill fell on Larry Mantell's foot. Larry jumped up suddenly and punched Henry Moore and pushed him into the wall. Henry may have suffered a concussion as a result of falling.

Questions 21-25.

DIRECTIONS: Answer Questions 21 through 25 *only* on the basis of the information provided in the following passage.

    A written report is a communication of information from one person to another. It is an account of some matter especially investigated, however routine that matter may be. The ultimate basis of any good written report is facts, which become known through observation and verification. Good written reports may seem to be no more than general ideas and opinions. However, in such cases, the facts leading to these opinions were gathered, verified, and reported earlier, and the opinions are dependent upon these facts. Good style, proper form and emphasis cannot make a good written report out of unreliable information and bad judgment; but, on the other hand, solid investigation and brilliant thinking are not likely to become very useful until they are effectively communicated to others. If a person's work calls for written reports, then his work is often no better than his written reports.

21. Based on the information in the passage, it can be concluded that opinions expressed in a report should be   21. ___

    A. based on facts which are gathered and reported
    B. emphasized repeatedly when they result from a special investigation
    C. kept to a minimum
    D. separated from the body of the report

22. In the above passage, the one of the following which is mentioned as a way of establishing facts is   22. ___

    A. authority   B. communication
    C. reporting   D. verification

23. According to the passage, the characteristic shared by *all* written reports is that they are   23. ___

    A. accounts of routine matters
    B. transmissions of information
    C. reliable and logical
    D. written in proper form

24. Which of the following conclusions can *logically* be drawn from the information given in the passage?

    A. Brilliant thinking can make up for unreliable information in a report.
    B. One method of judging an individual's work is the quality of the written reports he is required to submit.
    C. Proper form and emphasis can make a good report out of unreliable information.
    D. Good written reports that seem to be no more than general ideas should be rewritten.

25. Which of the following suggested titles would be *MOST* appropriate for this passage?

    A. Gathering and Organizing Facts
    B. Techniques of Observation
    C. Nature and Purpose of Reports
    D. Reports and Opinions: Differences and Similarities

KEY (CORRECT ANSWERS)

1. A		11. C
2. A		12. C
3. D		13. A
4. B		14. D
5. A		15. A
6. C		16. D
7. A		17. D
8. D		18. C
9. C		19. B
10. D		20. B

21.	A
22.	D
23.	B
24.	B
25.	C

TEST 3

Questions 1-5.

DIRECTIONS: The following is an accident report similar to those used in departments for reporting accidents. Answer Questions 1 to 5 using *only* the information given in this report.

ACCIDENT REPORT

FROM John Doe **TITLE** Sanitation Man	**DATE OF REPORT** June 23
DATE OF ACCIDENT June 22 time 3 AM PM **PLACE** 1489 Third Avenue	**CITY** Metropolitan
VEHICLE NO. 1	**VEHICLE NO. 2**
OPERATOR John Doe, Sanitation Man TITLE	**OPERATOR** Richard Roe
VEHICLE CODE NO. 14-238	**ADDRESS** 498 High Street
LICENSE NO. 0123456	**OWNER** Henry Roe **ADDRESS** 786 E. 83 St **LIC NUMBER** 5N1492

DESCRIPTION OF ACCIDENT Light green Chevrolet sedan while trying to pass drove in to rear side of Sanitation truck which had stopped to collect garbage. No one was injured but there was property damage.

NATURE OF DAMAGE TO PRIVATE VEHICLE Right front fender crushed, bumper bent.

DAMAGE TO CITY VEHICLE Front of left rear fender pushed in. Paint scraped.

NAME OF WITNESS Frank Brown	**ADRESS** 48 Kingsway
John Doe **Signature of person making this report**	**BADGE NO. 428**

1. Of the following, the one which has been omitted from this accident report is the   1. ___

     A.   location of the accident
     B.   drivers of the vehicles involved
     C.   traffic situation at the time of the accident
     D.   owners of the vehicles involved

2. The address of the driver of Vehicle No. 1 is not required because he   2. ___

     A.   is employed by the department
     B.   is not the owner of the vehicle
     C.   reported the accident
     D.   was injured in the accident

3. The report indicates that the driver of Vehicle No. 2 was *probably*

    A.   passing on the wrong side of the truck
    B.   not wearing his glasses
    C.   not injured in the accident
    D.   driving while intoxicated

4. The number of people *specifically* referred to in this report is

    A. 3   B. 4   C. 5   D. 6

5. The license number of Vehicle No. 1 is

    A. 428   B. 5N1492   C. 14-238   D. 0123456

6. In a report of unlawful entry into department premises, it is *LEAST* important to include the

    A.   estimated value of the property missing
    B.   general description of the premises
    C.   means used to get into the premises
    D.   time and date of entry

7. In a report of an accident, it is *LEAST* important to include the

    A.   name of the insurance company of the person injured in the accident
    B.   probable cause of the accident
    C.   time and place of the accident
    D.   names and addresses of all witnesses of the accident

8. Of the following, the one which is_____ *NOT* required in the preparation of a weekly functional expense report is the

    A.   hourly distribution of the time by proper heading in accordance with the actual work performed
    B.   signatures of officers not involved in the preparation of the report
    C.   time records of the men who appear on the payroll of the respective locations
    D.   time records of men working in other districts assigned to this location

---

KEY (CORRECT ANSWERS)

1.	C	5.	D
2.	A	6.	B
3.	C	7.	A
4.	B	8.	B

READING COMPREHENSION
UNDERSTANDING AND INTERPRETING WRITTEN MATERIAL
EXAMINATION SECTION
TEST 1

DIRECTIONS: Each question or incomplete statement is followed by several suggested answers or completions. Select the one that BEST answers the question or completes the statement. *PRINT THE LETTER OF THE CORRECT ANSWER IN THE SPACE AT THE RIGHT.*

Questions 1-8.

DIRECTIONS: Questions 1 through 8 are to be answered SOLELY on the basis of the information given in the following passage.

Machine flushing is the process of washing the street and forcibly pushing the street dirt toward the curbs by directing streams of water under pressure onto the surface of the street from a moving vehicle. Flushers have been known to clean as little as 1 1/2 miles and as much as 41 miles of street during a single 8 hour shift. The average for an 8 hour shift, as shown in a survey made of 36 cities, is 22 miles. The rather large variance is due to wide ranges in operating speeds of the flushers.

The number of shifts that are operated varies considerably among cities. Small communities usually are able to do the required cleaning in a single shift. Most of the larger cities, on the other hand, operate two shifts, and New York City has three shifts daily. New York City also has used chlorinated sea water during water shortages.

As in other kinds of cleaning, the work should be done when traffic is lightest. Parked vehicles do not significantly interfere with flushing, although a better job is done when there are but few cars standing at the curbs.

Flushers are particularly effective when the pavements are wet during and after rains. The rain softens the dirt, and the flushing water moves it away more easily. Substantially less water is required when pavements are wet, and the flushers can travel faster without decreasing their effectiveness. However, since the average citizen is not aware of these advantages, care should be exercised lest the impression be given that the city is watering the lawn while it is raining.

Flushers should not be used in freezing weather or when the temperature is near the freezing point. They may cause icy surfaces to form, thereby increasing the chances of traffic accidents. Therefore, water should never be used on pavements unless it is certain that it can evaporate or run off before it freezes.

1. Based on the information in the above passage, it is reasonable to assume that the MAIN reason for using water under pressure in machine flushing is to
    A. prevent wasting of water during shortages
    B. move the dirt to the curb
    C. make sure that the street is thoroughly wet
    D. clear the dirt that is at the curb

1.___

2. Based on the information in the above passage, a flusher   2. __
    that cleans 72 miles of street during a 16 hour period is
    operating at a rate _____ average.
        A. well above the   B. exactly
        C. slightly less than   D. well below the

3. According to the above passage, if there are a few cars   3. __
    standing at the curb when machine flushing is being done,
    the cleaning job
        A. can still be done adequately
        B. will be as effective as when there are many cars
           parked at the curb
        C. will be better than if there are no cars parked at
           the curb
        D. will be done poorly

4. Based on the information in the above passage, which one   4. __
    of the following is the MOST probable reason why New York
    City has three shifts daily for machine flushing operations?
        A. There is more personnel available for use in New York
           City.
        B. New York City has more water available than other
           cities.
        C. New York City's budget allows more money for flushing
           operations.
        D. All the necessary cleaning can't be done with fewer
           shifts.

5. According to the above passage, the flushing of streets   5. __
    during rain may
        A. take longer than street flushing in dry weather
        B. look like a poor practice to the public
        C. decrease the effectiveness of flushing operations
        D. cause a substantial waste of water

6. In the above passage, which of the following is NOT   6. __
    offered as an advantage of flushing streets when they are
    wet?
        A. Street dirt more pliable
        B. Street dirt easier to move
        C. Flusher can move faster
        D. Fewer pedestrians and traffic

7. As used in the above passage, the phrase *watering the lawn*   7. __
    while it is raining means to imply that the city is
        A. trying to impress the public
        B. not aware of the opinions of the average citizen
        C. giving its lawns too much water
        D. doing something unnecessary

8. According to the above passage, flushers should NOT be   8. __
    used in freezing weather because
        A. the water may freeze inside the flushers
        B. slippery driving conditions may be created
        C. evaporation or run-off of the water from the pavement
           is likely
        D. flushers can't move on icy surfaces

Questions 9-11.

DIRECTIONS: Questions 9 through 11 are to be answered SOLELY on the basis of the following paragraphs.

TYPES OF FILL

Any type of mineral earth or rock can be used as road fill, but clay and silt are generally undesirable. They soften when wet, frequently with changes in volume, and may act as a wick to bring ground water to the surface. Humus is avoided, particularly in its pure state, because of lack of bearing strength and excessive water absorption. Topsoil, a mixture of mineral soil and humus, may or may not be permissible, depending on its qualities and its location in the fill.

Sand and loose, clean gravel have excellent bearing power but afford poor traction, are hard to compact, and must be held in by other materials.

The most desirable fills are mixtures of two or more simple types. Varying proportions of clay, silt, sand, gravel, and stones are found in loams, boulder clay, and glacial till. Sand and gravel are most desirable when mixed with enough clay or silt to bind them together.

Light soils with a high percentage of sand or gravel are desirable when work must be done in rainy places or seasons. They absorb and drain off large quantities of water, and do not get slippery easily.

9. According to the above paragraphs, one of the reasons why   9.___
    sand alone is NOT a good material for fill is that sand
       A. is difficult to obtain   B. is hard to compact
       C. has poor bearing power   D. is expensive to purchase

10. According to the above paragraphs, the one of the following 10.___
     soils that is BEST for fills is
        A. clay
        B. humus
        C. gravel
        D. a mixture of sand, gravel, and clay

11. In rainy weather, the BEST type of fill material to work   11.___
     with is one containing a high percentage of
        A. clay   B. silt   C. gravel   D. humus

Questions 12-15.

DIRECTIONS: Questions 12 through 15 are to be answered SOLELY on the
              basis of the following paragraph. Each question consis
              of a statement. You are to indicate whether the stateme
              is TRUE (T) or FALSE (F).

The number of containers picked up per mile is a better index o
the labor requirements for the pick-up operation than the number of
houses served per mile. The labor time needed to collect refuse ove
a given distance increases in direct proportion to the number of
containers which must be lifted. It has been found that the number
of houses serviced per mile is quite adequate as an index of labor
requirements in those cities where the garbage and domestic refuse
is deposited in a single standard container and the practice is
enforced by law, but in such cases the number of houses serviced is
equal to the number of containers picked up.

12.   The greater the number of containers of refuse which must   12.
      be lifted within a given distance traveled, the greater
      the labor time required to collect the refuse over the
      distance.

13.   The number of houses serviced per mile sometimes equals   13.
      the number of containers picked up per mile by the
      collector.

14.   The number of houses serviced per mile is not an adequate   14.
      index of the labor requirements for the pick-up operation
      in any city.

15.   In those cities where the practice of depositing garbage   15.
      and domestic refuse in separate standard containers is
      enforced by law, the number of houses serviced per mile
      is a good index of labor requirements.

Questions 16-21.

DIRECTIONS: Questions 16 through 21 are to be answered SOLELY on
              the basis of the following paragraph. Each question
              consists of a statement. You are to indicate whether
              the statement is TRUE (T) or FALSE (F).

Those unplanned and undesirable occurrences which injure people
destroy equipment and materials, interrupt the orderly progress of
any activity, or waste time and money are called accidents. Some
degree of hazard is associated with every form of activity, and
every uncontrolled hazard will in time produce its share of accidents. Accidents do not just happen. They are caused by unsafe
conditions or unsafe acts or both. A safety program is an organized
effort to eliminate physical hazards and unsafe practices in order
to prevent accidents and their resultant injuries. Safety is not
something to be thought of only when no other duties are pressing,
but must become part of every activity of every day.

16. A happening that is not wanted and not planned and wastes   16.____
    time and money is called an accident.

17. There is no activity that is free of hazard.   17.____

18. Hazardous conditions are uncontrollable.   18.____

19. An accident will not happen if the physical conditions   19.____
    are safe.

20. A safety program seeks to prevent accidents by getting   20.____
    rid of unsafe practices and physical hazards.

21. Safety is apart from every day activities.   21.____

Questions 22-25.

DIRECTIONS: Questions 22 through 25 are to be answered SOLELY on
               the basis of the following paragraph. Each question
               consists of a statement. You are to indicate whether
               the statement is TRUE (T) or FALSE (F).

       In a comparison made between collection by means of open-body
trucks and collection by means of mechanical packers, it was found
that refuse collectors working with mechanical compaction trucks
spent approximately seven percent of the pick-up time in waiting.
Only two percent of the pick-up time was consumed by collectors
in waiting in the case of collection by open-body trucks.

22. In the comparison made, more than one type of truck was   22.____
    used.

23. A mechanical compaction truck travels more slowly than   23.____
    an open-body truck.

24. A comparison indicates that collectors spend a smaller   24.____
    percentage of pick-up time in waiting when they work with
    open-body trucks than when they work with mechanical
    compaction trucks.

25. In refuse collection, type of truck used is a factor   25.____
    influencing time spent on one element of the operation.

———

KEY (CORRECT ANSWERS)

1. B	6. D	11. C	16. T	21. F
2. A	7. D	12. T	17. T	22. T
3. A	8. B	13. T	18. F	23. F
4. D	9. B	14. F	19. F	24. T
5. B	10. D	15. F	20. T	25. T

———

TEST 2

Questions 1-6.

There is no other service offered by a community in which there
is such intimate contact with the individual citizen as in the refuse
collection service. Because of this intimate contact, it is vitally
important that each sanitation man in the service have the proper
public relations attitude.

He should be imbued with a genuine desire to provide good
service. This service should be impartial, performed in a neat and
efficient manner, and the employee should be competent, willing, and
efficient.

Every employee in the refuse collection service should be
trained in contacting the public whether his job calls for contact
in person, by telephone, or by letter. All requests for information
and all complaints should be acknowledged promptly and courteously.
If practicable, a personal contact should then be made. Later, if
necessary, this should be followed up by a proper written reply.
Decisions should be backed by the logic of operational problems
rather than by flat recitals of codes, ordinances, or rules. But
more important than the settling of complaints is the carrying out
of the work in such a manner as to eliminate the causes of complaints in the beginning. The chief causes of complaints are the
rough handling of containers, spillage of refuse, damage to lawns
and shrubbery by collectors, and incomplete removal service. These
complaints can be minimized by the training of personnel and by
instilling in them a desire to do a good job. The training of
drivers to operate their equipment properly is also important. The
impression which city equipment makes on the citizen depends on
its use as well as on its appearance. A reckless driver or an
inconsiderate driver is not liked under any circumstance, but if
he is driving a municipal vehicle, his offense is doubly magnified.
A driver training program will pay dividends not only in improved
public relations but in reduced costs.

1. According to the above passage, the MAIN reason why it   1
   is important for a sanitation man to have a good public
   relations attitude is that
   A. refuse collection affects the community's health
   B. his work will be improved
   C. he is in close touch with the private citizen
   D. he is offering an important community service

2. According to the above passage, after a complaint about the refuse collection service is acknowledged, it is desirable NEXT to
    A. make an investigation
    B. make a decision about the complaint
    C. interview the complainant in person
    D. follow up with a letter

2.___

3. According to the above passage, if a sanitation man has to make a decision in answer to a complaint from a citizen, it would be BEST for him to explain to the complainant
    A. why refuse collection operations make this decision necessary
    B. the reason for the decision by referring to the appropriate rules
    C. the local code which justifies the decision
    D. how the cause of the complaint might have been eliminated in the beginning

3.___

4. Based on the above passage, it is reasonable to assume that when a sanitation man is assigned to handle requests for information or complaints about the refuse collection service, he should
    A. give first attention to complaints
    B. give first attention to requests for information
    C. handle both complaints and information requests quickly
    D. handle first whatever he has the greatest number of

4.___

5. According to the above passage, the one of the following which does NOT seem to be a main source of complaints by the public about the refuse collection service is
    A. some material put out for collection being left over
    B. noise of collectors
    C. dirtying of the collection area
    D. damage to property

5.___

6. According to the above passage, the public's reaction to a poor driver is
    A. the same no matter what vehicle he is driving
    B. more severe if the vehicle involved is in poor condition
    C. more severe if he turns out to be a municipal employee
    D. more severe if he is operating city equipment

6.___

Questions 7-9.

DIRECTIONS: Questions 7 through 9 should be answered ONLY on the basis of the following passage.

A heavy snowfall may cause delays in the movement of trains and buses. People are often late for work when it snows. Both pedestrians and cars have accidents because of snow and ice. Pedestrians slip and fall. Cars skid and collide.

7. The above passage indicates that heavy snow   7.___
   A. is a beautiful thing to see
   B. may make the trains run late
   C. gives temporary work to the unemployed
   D. should be cleared from sidewalks within four hours

8. According to the above passage, snow and ice may cause   8.___
   cars to
   A. slow down B. freeze   C. stall   D. skid

9. The above passage says that when it snows,   9.___
   A. children love to have snowball fights
   B. people are often late for work
   C. garbage collection is halted
   D. snow plows must be attached to garbage trucks

Questions 10-11.

DIRECTIONS: Questions 10 and 11 are to be answered ONLY on the
              basis of the following passage.

     It would be unusual for a snowstorm to develop without warning.
When a warning is received, sanitation men load the salt spreaders
and attach plows to the trucks.

10. According to the passage, a snowstorm seldom develops   10.___
    A. without advance notice
    B. in the spring
    C. in the city
    D. without rain coming first

11. Once a snow warning is received, sanitation men prepare   11.___
    for the storm by
    A. removing plows from the trucks
    B. greasing and oiling the salt spreaders
    C. emptying the salt spreaders
    D. putting plows on the trucks

Questions 12-14.

DIRECTIONS: Questions 12 through 14 are to be answered ONLY on the
              basis of the following passage.

     Helping to prevent accidents is the job of every worker.
Foremen should be told about unsafe equipment right away. Workers
should wear safe clothing. Knees should be bent when lifting, and
help should be enlisted when picking up heavy objects.

12. The above passage says that helping to prevent accidents   12.___
    is the job of
    A. the foreman   B. the safety division
    C. management   D. every worker

13. Equipment that is not safe should be   13.____
    A. used with special care
    B. reported to the foreman right away
    C. marked with a red tag
    D. parked at the side of the road

14. When lifting very heavy objects, the worker should   14.____
    A. ask the foreman to see what is being done
    B. keep legs straight
    C. always wear protective gloves
    D. get help to assist him

Questions 15-17.

DIRECTIONS: Questions 15 through 17 are to be answered ONLY on the
basis of the information in the following passage.

Sanitation men sometimes have to listen to complaints from the
public. When an angry citizen complains, the supervisor should
remember to stay calm. If possible, the complaint should be
answered. If the supervisor cannot answer the complaint, the
complainant should be referred to someone who can answer it.

15. Sanitation men who come into contact with the public   15.____
sometimes have to
    A. sweep up trash   B. shout at citizens
    C. listen to complaints   D. help put out fires

16. If a citizen who is complaining to the worker is very   16.____
angry, the worker should
    A. get angry   B. stay calm
    C. ignore him   D. none of the above

17. If the worker cannot answer the complaint, he should   17.____
    A. make up something that sounds logical
    B. ask a passer-by for the information
    C. tell the complainant who can give him the answer
    D. tell the complainant he does not know and walk away

Questions 18-19.

DIRECTIONS: Questions 18 and 19 are to be answered ONLY on the basis
of the following passage.

The Department of Sanitation starts early in the month of May
to prepare for snow expected during the following winter. It begins
by fixing the snow removal equipment which was used during the
winter. It is then usually kept busy with either snow removal or
preparation for snow removal every month through the end of March.

18. According to the above passage, for how many months during   18.____
the year is the Department of Sanitation busy with either
snow removal or preparation for snow removal?
    A. 9   B. 10   C. 11   D. 12

19. According to the passage, in the month of May, the   19.___
    Department of Sanitation
    A. stores the snow removal equipment
    B. fixes the snow removal equipment
    C. equips the sanitation men
    D. collects the garbage piled up because of snow

Questions 20-22.

DIRECTIONS: Questions 20 through 22 are to be answered ONLY on the
              basis of the paragraph below.

     In an open discussion designed to arrive at solutions to
community problems, the person leading the discussion group should
give the members a chance to make their suggestions before he makes
his. He must not be afraid of silence. If he talks just to keep
things going, he will find he can't stop, and good discussion will
not develop. In other words, the more he talks, the more the group
will depend on him. If he finds, however, that no one seems ready
to begin the discussion, his best *opening* is to ask for definitions
of terms which form the basis of the discussion. By pulling out as
many definitions or interpretations as possible, he can get the group
started *thinking out loud*, which is essential to good discussion.

20. According to the passage above, good group discussion is   20.___
    most likely to result if the person leading the discussion
    group
    A. keeps the discussion going by speaking whenever the
       group stops speaking
    B. encourages the group to depend on him by speaking
       more than any other group member
    C. makes his own suggestions before the group has a
       chance to make theirs
    D. encourages discussion by asking the group to interpret
       the terms to be discussed

21. According to the paragraph above, *thinking out loud* by   21.___
    the discussion group is
    A. *good* practice because *thinking out loud* is important
       to good discussion
    B. *poor* practice because group members should think out
       their ideas before discussing them
    C. *good* practice because it will encourage the person
       leading the discussion to speak more
    D. *poor* practice because it causes the group to fear
       silence during a discussion

22. According to the paragraph above, the one of the   22.___
    following which is LEAST desirable at an open discussion
    is having
    A. silent periods during which none of the group members
       speaks
    B. differences of opinion among the group members
       concerning the definition of terms

C. a discussion leader who uses *openings* to get the discussion started
D. a discussion leader who provides all suggestions and definitions for the group

Questions 23-24.

DIRECTIONS: Questions 23 and 24 are to be answered ONLY on the basis of the paragraph below.

When a written report must be submitted by a foreman to his supervisor, the best rule is *the briefer the better*. Obviously, this can be carried to extremes since all necessary information must be included. However, the ability to write a satisfactory one-page report is an important communication skill. There are many types of reports a foreman must submit to his supervisor. One is the form report, which is printed and merely requires the foreman to fill in blanks. The greatest problem faced in completion of this report is accuracy and thoroughness. Another type of report is one that must be submitted regularly and systematically. This type of report is known as the periodic report.

23. According to the passage above, accuracy and thoroughness   23.___
    are the GREATEST problems in the completion of ____ reports.
    A. one-page   B. form   C. periodic   D. long

24. According to the passage above, a good written report from   24.___
    a foreman to his supervisor should GENERALLY be
    A. printed   B. periodic   C. brief   D. formal

Question 25.

DIRECTIONS: Question 25 is to be answered ONLY on the basis of the paragraph below.

Since metering reduces water waste considerably, daily operating costs are similarly reduced. Less water pumped means less expense for power to run pumps, less chemicals for treatment, less overall overhead and operating expense.

25. According to the above paragraph, the one of the following   25.___
    statements that is CORRECT is:
    A. Water is chemically treated in order to save power
    B. Water is chemically treated in order to save on overhead
    C. Metering of water means that more water must be pumped
    D. Metering of water results in less overall overhead and operating expenses

KEY (CORRECT ANSWERS)

1.	C	11.	D
2.	C	12.	D
3.	A	13.	B
4.	C	14.	D
5.	B	15.	C
6.	D	16.	B
7.	B	17.	C
8.	D	18.	C
9.	B	19.	B
10.	A	20.	D

21. A
22. D
23. B
24. C
25. D

TEST 3

RESCUE BREATHING

Mouth-to-mouth, or rescue breathing, is the easiest, most
efficient and quickest method of getting oxygen into a suffocating
victim of drowning, heart attack, electrical shock, poisoning, or
other cause of interruption of breathing. It is superior to other
types of artificial respiration because the victim does not have to
be moved, and the rescuer can continue for hours without exhaustion.
No special equipment is needed.

Begin rescue breathing immediately. The victim's head should
be lower than his body. Tilt his head back as far as possible so
his jaw juts out. Keep the air passage to his lungs straight at all
times. Open your mouth as wide as possible, and seal your lips over
the adult victim's mouth or his nose and the child victim's mouth
and nose. Blow in air until his chest rises. Remove your mouth and
listen to him breathe out. Then blow again and fill his lungs.

For the first minute, blow thirty times into a child, then twenty
times a minute. With an adult, blow twenty times for the first minute
then ten to twelve times a minute. Do not stop breathing for the
victim, however long it takes, until he begins breathing for himself --
or is dead.

1. The fastest way to get oxygen into the lungs of a suffocating   1.____
    person is by mouth-to-mouth breathing.

2. The rescue breathing method of artificial respiration should   2.____
    be used only in cases of drowning.

3. Rescue breathing is not the only kind of artificial   3.____
    respiration.

4. The person who applies mouth-to-mouth breathing will not   4.____
    tire easily.

5. Special equipment used in rescue breathing should be kept   5.____
    handy at all times.

6. Rescue breathing should be commenced at the earliest possible moment.   6

7. The suffocating victim should be placed so that his body is not higher than his head.   7

8. In rescue breathing, the head of the victim should be bent forward so oxygen will be more easily forced into his lungs.   8

9. In mouth-to-mouth breathing, air may be blown into the victim's nose.   9

10. When rescue breathing is applied to children, air should be blown into the lungs thirty times during the first minute.   10

11. It is never necessary to continue rescue breathing for longer than about five minutes.   11

12. Mouth-to-mouth breathing is always successful in reviving the victim.   12

Questions 13-16.

DIRECTIONS: Questions 13 through 16 are to be answered ONLY on the basis of the information contained in the following paragraph.

Standardizing the size of a satisfactory refuse container may determine how often refuse is collected. A standard size is arrived at by considering the ease of handling the can and the average rate of accumulation of the refuse at the household. An excessive amount of refuse at the household should be avoided as it invariably leads to inferior sanitation practices.

13. The frequency of refuse collection may be influenced by the size of the refuse container.   13.

14. Ease of handling a refuse can is a factor in arriving at a standard size for a refuse container.   14.

15. The cause of poorer sanitation practices is invariably excessive piling up of refuse at the household.   15.

16. Excessive production of refuse at the household should be prevented.   16.

Questions 17-22.

DIRECTIONS: Questions 17 through 22 are to be answered ONLY on the basis of the information contained in the following paragraph.

It is possible for an inspection program of sanitation equipment to contribute toward the maximum utilization of equipment only if the inspections are properly scheduled, performed, and acted upon. This is so because the maximum utilization of equipment depends on a number of factors. A long life span for the equipment must be obtained by proper maintenance and repair. Organization and scheduling the manpower and equipment must be directed toward preventing the equipment from remaining unnecessarily idle. The maximum period of time for the use of any piece of motor equipment is that interval between the instant the equipment is received and the moment it becomes obsolete, the interval of availability. The purpose of an inspection program is to help expand the volume of work accomplished by equipment within the interval of availability, which in modern times is rapidly contracting.

17. If inspections of sanitation equipment are properly scheduled, performed, and acted upon, they insure maximum utilization of equipment.   17.____

18. To get a long life span for the equipment, proper maintenance and repair are necessary.   18.____

19. Maximum use of manpower is obtained when there is maximum use of equipment.   19.____

20. The longest period of time possible for the use of a piece of motor equipment is the time between the moment it becomes obsolete and the instant it is received.   20.____

21. The purpose of an equipment inspection program is to help increase the volume of work produced by the equipment from the time the equipment is received until the time it becomes obsolete.   21.____

22. In modern times, the maximum period of time for the use of any piece of motor equipment is rapidly shrinking.   22.____

Questions 23-25.

DIRECTIONS: Questions 23 through 25, inclusive, are to be answered in accordance with the following paragraph. Each question or statement is followed by several suggested answers or completions. Select the one that BEST answers the question or completes the statement. *PRINT THE LETTER OF THE CORRECT ANSWER IN THE SPACE AT THE RIGHT.*

You have been instructed to expedite the fabrication of three special sand spreader trucks using chassis that are available in the shop. All three trucks must be completed by November 1, 1981. Based on workload and available hours, the foreman of the body shop indicates that he could manufacture one complete sand spreader body per month, with one additional week required for mounting and securing each body to the available chassis. No work could begin on the body until the engines and hydraulic components, which would have to be purchased, were available for use. The Purchasing Department has promised the delivery of engines and hydraulic components three months after the order is placed. (Assume that all months have four weeks, and the same crew is doing the assembling and manufacturing.)

23. With reference to the above paragraph, the LATEST date that   23
the engines and associated hydraulic components could be
requisitioned in order to meet the specified deadline would
be MOST NEARLY the end of the ____ week in ____ 1981.
   A. second; March   B. first; April
   C. first; May   D. first; June

24. With reference to the above paragraph, the date of   24
completion of the first sand spreader truck, assuming that
the Purchasing Department placed the order at the beginning
of the second week in February 1981 and ultimate delivery
of the engines and components was delayed by a month would
be MOST NEARLY the end of the ____ week in ____ 1981.
   A. second; June   B. fourth; June
   C. second; July   C. fourth; July

25. With reference to the above paragraph, the date of   25
completion of the last sand spreader truck, assuming that
the Purchasing Department placed the order at the beginning
of the second week in February 1981 and actual delivery of
the engines and components was made two weeks early, would
be MOST NEARLY the end of the ____ week in ____ 1981.
   A. second; August   B. first; September
   C. third; September   D. second; October

KEY (CORRECT ANSWERS)

1. T		11. F
2. F		12. F
3. T		13. T
4. T		14. T
5. F		15. F
6. T		16. F
7. F		17. F
8. F		18. T
9. T		19. F
10. T		20. T

21. T
22. T
23. B
24. C
25. A

ANSWER SHEET

NO. _____ PART _____ TITLE OF POSITION _____

(AS GIVEN IN EXAMINATION ANNOUNCEMENT - INCLUDE OPTION, IF ANY)

E OF EXAMINATION _____

(CITY OR TOWN)   (STATE)   DATE _____

RATING

USE THE SPECIAL PENCIL.   MAKE GLOSSY BLACK MARKS.

	A B C D E		A B C D E		A B C D E		A B C D E		A B C D E
1	:: :: :: :: ::	26	:: :: :: :: ::	51	:: :: :: :: ::	76	:: :: :: :: ::	101	:: :: :: :: ::
2	:: :: :: :: ::	27	:: :: :: :: ::	52	:: :: :: :: ::	77	:: :: :: :: ::	102	:: :: :: :: ::
3	:: :: :: :: ::	28	:: :: :: :: ::	53	:: :: :: :: ::	78	:: :: :: :: ::	103	:: :: :: :: ::
4	:: :: :: :: ::	29	:: :: :: :: ::	54	:: :: :: :: ::	79	:: :: :: :: ::	104	:: :: :: :: ::
5	:: :: :: :: ::	30	:: :: :: :: ::	55	:: :: :: :: ::	80	:: :: :: :: ::	105	:: :: :: :: ::
6	:: :: :: :: ::	31	:: :: :: :: ::	56	:: :: :: :: ::	81	:: :: :: :: ::	106	:: :: :: :: ::
7	:: :: :: :: ::	32	:: :: :: :: ::	57	:: :: :: :: ::	82	:: :: :: :: ::	107	:: :: :: :: ::
8	:: :: :: :: ::	33	:: :: :: :: ::	58	:: :: :: :: ::	83	:: :: :: :: ::	108	:: :: :: :: ::
9	:: :: :: :: ::	34	:: :: :: :: ::	59	:: :: :: :: ::	84	:: :: :: :: ::	109	:: :: :: :: ::
10	:: :: :: :: ::	35	:: :: :: :: ::	60	:: :: :: :: ::	85	:: :: :: :: ::	110	:: :: :: :: ::

Make only ONE mark for each answer.   Additional and stray marks may be
counted as mistakes.   In making corrections, erase errors COMPLETELY.

	A B C D E		A B C D E		A B C D E		A B C D E		A B C D E
11	:: :: :: :: ::	36	:: :: :: :: ::	61	:: :: :: :: ::	86	:: :: :: :: ::	111	:: :: :: :: ::
12	:: :: :: :: ::	37	:: :: :: :: ::	62	:: :: :: :: ::	87	:: :: :: :: ::	112	:: :: :: :: ::
13	:: :: :: :: ::	38	:: :: :: :: ::	63	:: :: :: :: ::	88	:: :: :: :: ::	113	:: :: :: :: ::
14	:: :: :: :: ::	39	:: :: :: :: ::	64	:: :: :: :: ::	89	:: :: :: :: ::	114	:: :: :: :: ::
15	:: :: :: :: ::	40	:: :: :: :: ::	65	:: :: :: :: ::	90	:: :: :: :: ::	115	:: :: :: :: ::
16	:: :: :: :: ::	41	:: :: :: :: ::	66	:: :: :: :: ::	91	:: :: :: :: ::	116	:: :: :: :: ::
17	:: :: :: :: ::	42	:: :: :: :: ::	67	:: :: :: :: ::	92	:: :: :: :: ::	117	:: :: :: :: ::
18	:: :: :: :: ::	43	:: :: :: :: ::	68	:: :: :: :: ::	93	:: :: :: :: ::	118	:: :: :: :: ::
19	:: :: :: :: ::	44	:: :: :: :: ::	69	:: :: :: :: ::	94	:: :: :: :: ::	119	:: :: :: :: ::
20	:: :: :: :: ::	45	:: :: :: :: ::	70	:: :: :: :: ::	95	:: :: :: :: ::	120	:: :: :: :: ::
21	:: :: :: :: ::	46	:: :: :: :: ::	71	:: :: :: :: ::	96	:: :: :: :: ::	121	:: :: :: :: ::
22	:: :: :: :: ::	47	:: :: :: :: ::	72	:: :: :: :: ::	97	:: :: :: :: ::	122	:: :: :: :: ::
23	:: :: :: :: ::	48	:: :: :: :: ::	73	:: :: :: :: ::	98	:: :: :: :: ::	123	:: :: :: :: ::
24	:: :: :: :: ::	49	:: :: :: :: ::	74	:: :: :: :: ::	99	:: :: :: :: ::	124	:: :: :: :: ::
25	:: :: :: :: ::	50	:: :: :: :: ::	75	:: :: :: :: ::	100	:: :: :: :: ::	125	:: :: :: :: ::

ANSWER SHEET

TEST NO. _____ PART _____ TITLE OF POSITION _____

(AS GIVEN IN EXAMINATION ANNOUNCEMENT - INCLUDE OPTION, IF ANY)

PLACE OF EXAMINATION _____ DATE _____

(CITY OR TOWN)　　　　　　　　　　　(STATE)

RATING

USE THE SPECIAL PENCIL.　MAKE GLOSSY BLACK MARKS.

	A	B	C	D	E			A	B	C	D	E			A	B	C	D	E			A	B	C	D	E			A	B	C	D	E
1							26							51							76							101					
2							27							52							77							102					
3							28							53							78							103					
4							29							54							79							104					
5							30							55							80							105					
6							31							56							81							106					
7							32							57							82							107					
8							33							58							83							108					
9							34							59							84							109					
10							35							60							85							110					

Make only ONE mark for each answer.　Additional and stray marks may be
counted as mistakes.　In making corrections, erase errors COMPLETELY.

	A	B	C	D	E			A	B	C	D	E			A	B	C	D	E			A	B	C	D	E			A	B	C	D	E
11							36							61							86							111					
12							37							62							87							112					
13							38							63							88							113					
14							39							64							89							114					
15							40							65							90							115					
16							41							66							91							116					
17							42							67							92							117					
18							43							68							93							118					
19							44							69							94							119					
20							45							70							95							120					
21							46							71							96							121					
22							47							72							97							122					
23							48							73							98							123					
24							49							74							99							124					
25							50							75							100							125					